GENERAL CONFERENCE ADDRESSES

___

GENERAL CONFERENCE ADDRESSES

JOURNAL EDITION
APRIL 2021

DESERET
BOOK

SALT LAKE CITY, UTAH

CONTENTS

PRIESTHOOD SESSION

SUNDAY MORNING SESSION

SUNDAY AFTERNOON SESSION

SATURDAY MORNING SESSION

APRIL 3, 2021

WELCOME MESSAGE

PRESIDENT RUSSELL M. NELSON

President of The Church of Jesus Christ of Latter-day Saints

My dear brothers and sisters and friends throughout the world, I offer my personal welcome to this general conference. We gather as a great global family desiring to worship our Lord and Savior, Jesus Christ. Thank you for joining with us.

This last year has been one for the record books. No doubt we have each learned things we did not know previously. Some lessons that I knew *before* have been written on my heart in new and instructive ways.

For example, I *know* for sure that the Lord directs the affairs of His Church. He said, "I will show [you] that I am able to do mine own work."[1]

Often, my counselors and I have watched through tear-brimmed eyes as He has interceded in extremely challenging circumstances after we had done our best and could do no more. We do indeed stand all amazed.

I also understand better now what He meant when He said, "Behold, I will hasten my work in its time."[2] Over and over again I have rejoiced as He has directed and executed the hastening of His work—even during a global pandemic.

My dear brothers and sisters, the strength of the Church lies in the efforts and ever-growing testimonies of its members. Testimonies are best cultivated in the home. During this past year, *many* of you have dramatically increased the study of the gospel in your homes. I thank you, and your children will thank you.

The huge project to renovate the Salt Lake Temple continues. From my office I have a front-row seat to watch the work taking place on the temple plaza.

As I have watched workers dig out old tree roots, plumbing, wiring, and a leaky fountain, I have thought about the need for each of us to remove, with the Savior's help, the old debris in our lives.

The gospel of Jesus Christ *is* a gospel of repentance.[3] Because of the Savior's Atonement, His gospel provides an invitation to keep changing, growing, and becoming more pure. It is a gospel of hope, of healing, and of progress. Thus, the gospel is a message of *joy*! Our spirits rejoice with every small step forward we take.

Part of the gathering of Israel, and a very important part, is the charge for us as a people to be *worthy* and *willing* to help prepare the world for the Second Coming of the Lord.

As we listen to the messages that have been carefully prepared by our leaders under the direction of the Holy Ghost, I invite you to pray to identify the debris you should remove from your life so you can become more worthy.

I love you, my dear brothers and sisters, and testify that our Heavenly Father and His Beloved Son know and love you individually. They stand ready to assist you in every step forward you take. Welcome to general conference and to the privilege of hearing the voice of the Lord. In the name of Jesus Christ, amen.

Notes

1. 2 Nephi 27:21.
2. Doctrine and Covenants 88:73.
3. See Doctrine and Covenants 13:1.

GOD AMONG US

ELDER DIETER F. UCHTDORF
Of the Quorum of the Twelve Apostles

Throughout the ages, God has spoken through His servants, the prophets.[1] This morning we have had the privilege to hear the prophet of God speak to all the world. We love you, President Nelson, and I encourage everyone everywhere to study and heed your words.

Before I reached my 12th birthday, our family had been forced twice to flee our home and start over amid the chaos, fear, and uncertainties caused by war and political division. It was an anxious time for me, but it must have been terrifying for my beloved parents.

My mother and father shared little about this burden with us four children. They bore the strain and suffering as best they could. The fear must have been oppressive, consuming their hours and dampening their hope.

This time of bleakness after World War II left its mark upon the world. It left its mark upon me.

Back then, in the solitude of my loneliest hours, I often wondered, "Is there any hope left in the world?"

Angels among Us

As I pondered this question, I thought about our young American missionaries who served among us during those years. They had left the safety of their homes half a world away and traveled to Germany—land of their recent enemies—to offer divine hope to our people. They came not to blame, lecture, or shame. They willingly gave of their young lives without thought of earthly gain, wanting only to help others find the joy and peace they had experienced.

To me, these young men and women were perfect. I am sure they had flaws, but not to me. I will always think of them as being bigger than life—angels of light and glory, ministers of compassion, goodness, and truth.

While the world was drowning in cynicism, bitterness, hatred, and fear, the example and teachings of these young people filled me with hope. The gospel message they offered transcended politics, history, grudges, grievances, and personal agendas. It gave divine answers to important questions we had during these difficult times.

The message was that God lived and cared about us, even in these hours of turmoil, confusion, and chaos. That He actually appeared in our time to restore truth and light—His gospel and His Church. That He speaks to prophets again; that God is among us—and is personally involved in our lives and actively guiding His children.

It is astonishing what we can learn when we look a little closer at our Heavenly Father's plan of salvation and exaltation, the plan of happiness, for His children. When we feel insignificant, cast off, and forgotten, we learn that we may be assured that God has not forgotten us—in fact, that He offers to all His children something unimaginable: to become "heirs of God, and joint-heirs with Christ."[2]

What does this mean?

That we will live forever, receive a fulness of joy,[3] and have the potential to "inherit thrones, kingdoms, principalities, and powers."[4]

It is so humbling to know that this magnificent and supernal future is possible—not because of who we are but because of who God is.

Knowing this, how could we ever murmur or remain embittered? How could we ever keep our eyes on the ground when the King of kings invites us to take flight into an unimaginable future of divine happiness?[5]

Salvation among Us

Because of God's perfect love for us and the eternal sacrifice of Jesus Christ, our sins—both great and small—can be blotted out and remembered no more.[6] We can stand before Him pure, worthy, and sanctified.

My heart overflows with gratitude for my Heavenly Father. I realize that He has not doomed His children to stumble through mortality without hope for a bright and eternal future. He has provided instructions that reveal the way back to Him. And at the center of it all is *His Beloved Son, Jesus Christ*,[7] and His sacrifice for us.

The Savior's infinite Atonement completely changes the way we may view our transgressions and imperfections. Instead of dwelling on them and feeling irredeemable or hopeless, we can learn from them and feel hopeful.[8] The cleansing gift of repentance allows us to leave our sins behind and emerge a new creature.[9]

Because of Jesus Christ, our failures do not have to define us. They can refine us.

Like a musician rehearsing scales, we can see our missteps, flaws, and sins as opportunities for greater self-awareness, deeper and more honest love for others, and refinement through repentance.

If we repent, mistakes do not disqualify us. They are part of our progress.

We are all infants compared to the beings of glory and grandeur we are designed to become. No mortal being advances from crawling to walking to running without frequent stumbles, bumps, and bruises. That is how we learn.

If we earnestly keep practicing, always striving to keep God's commandments, and committing our efforts to repenting, enduring, and applying what we learn, line upon line, we will gather light into our souls.[10] And though we may not fully comprehend our full potential now, "we know that, when [the Savior] shall appear," we will see His countenance in us and "shall see him as he is."[11]

What a glorious promise!

Yes, the world is in turmoil. And yes, we have weaknesses. But we do not need to hang our heads in despair, because we can trust God, we can trust His Son, Jesus Christ, and we can accept the gift of the Spirit to guide us on this path toward a life filled with joy and divine happiness.[12]

Jesus among Us

I often have wondered, What would Jesus teach and do if He were among us today?

After the Resurrection, Jesus Christ fulfilled His promise to visit His "other sheep."[13]

The Book of Mormon: Another Testament of Jesus Christ speaks of such an appearance to the people on the American continent. We have this precious record as a tangible witness of the Savior's work.

The people of the Book of Mormon lived on the other side of the globe—their histories, cultures, and political climates were vastly different from the people Jesus taught during His mortal ministry. And yet He taught them many of the same things He taught in the Holy Land.

Why would He do that?

The Savior always teaches timeless truths. They apply to people of every age and in any circumstance.

His message was and is a message of hope and belonging—a testimony that God our Heavenly Father has not abandoned His children.

That God is among us!

Two hundred years ago, the Savior again returned to earth. Together with God the Father, He appeared to a 14-year-old Joseph Smith and ushered in the Restoration of the gospel and the Church of Jesus Christ. From that day forward, the heavens opened, and heavenly messengers descended from halls of immortal glory. Light and knowledge poured forth from the celestial throne.

The Lord Jesus Christ spoke once again to the world.

What did He say?

To our blessing, many of His words are recorded in the Doctrine and Covenants—available to anyone in the world who wishes to read and study them. How priceless are these words to us today!

And we should not be surprised to find that the Savior again teaches the core message of His gospel: "Thou shalt love the Lord thy God with all thy heart, with all thy might, mind, and strength; and in the name of Jesus Christ thou shalt serve him."[14] He inspires us to seek God[15] and live by the teachings He has revealed to His servants, the prophets.[16]

He teaches us to love one another[17] and to be "full of charity towards all men."[18]

He invites us to be His hands, to go about doing good.[19] "Let us not love in word . . . but in deed and in truth."[20]

He challenges us to heed His great commission: to love, to share, to invite all to His gospel and His Church.[21]

He commands us to build holy temples and to enter and serve there.[22]

He teaches us to become His disciples—that our hearts should not strive for personal power, wealth, approval, or position. He teaches us to "lay aside the things of this world, and seek for the things of a better."[23]

He urges us to seek joy, enlightenment, peace, truth, happiness,[24] and the promise of immortality and eternal life.[25]

Let us take this a step further. Suppose Jesus came to your ward, to your branch, or to your home today. What would that be like?

He would see right into your heart. Outward appearances would lose their importance. He would know you as you are. He would know your heart's desires.

The meek and the humble He would lift.

The sick He would heal.

The doubting He would infuse with faith and courage to believe.

He would teach us to open our hearts to God and reach out to others.

He would recognize and honor honesty, humility, integrity, faithfulness, compassion, and charity.

One look into His eyes and we would never be the same. We would be forever changed. Transformed by the profound realization that, indeed, God is among us.

What Shall We Do?[26]

I look back with kindness on the young man I was during my growing-up years. If I could go back in time, I would comfort him and tell him to stay on the right track and keep searching. And I would ask him to invite Jesus Christ into his life, for God is among us!

To you, my dear brothers and sisters, my dear friends, and to all who are searching for answers, truth, and happiness, I do offer the same counsel: keep searching with faith and patience.[27]

Ask, and you will receive. Knock, and it will be opened unto you.[28] Trust the Lord.[29]

In our daily life it is our paramount task and blessed opportunity to encounter God.

As we set aside pride and approach His throne with a broken heart and a contrite spirit,[30] He will draw near to us.[31]

As we seek to follow Jesus Christ and walk the path of discipleship, line upon line, the day will come that we will experience that unimaginable gift of receiving a fulness of joy.

My beloved friends, your Heavenly Father loves you with a perfect love. He has proven His love in endless ways, but above all by giving His Only Begotten Son as a sacrifice and as a gift to His children to make the return to our heavenly parents a reality.

I bear witness that our Heavenly Father lives, that Jesus Christ leads His Church, that President Russell M. Nelson is His prophet.

I extend to you my love and blessing at this joyful Easter season. Open your hearts to our Savior and Redeemer, no matter your circumstances, trials, sufferings, or mistakes; you can know that He lives, that He loves you, and that because of Him, you will never be alone.

God is among us.

Of this I testify and bear witness in the sacred name of Jesus Christ, amen.

Notes

1. See Amos 3:7.
2. Romans 8:17; see also Doctrine and Covenants 84:38.
3. See 3 Nephi 28:10.
4. Doctrine and Covenants 132:19.
5. See Alma 28:12; Mormon 7:7.
6. The words of Doctrine and Covenants 58:42 are some of the most inspiring and encouraging in scripture: "He who has repented of his sins, the same is forgiven, and I, the Lord, remember them no more." What joy this gives me to know that if I continue to repent, in that future day

when I shall fall on my knees before my Savior and Redeemer, He will lift me up and embrace me. My sins will not only be forgiven; they will not even be remembered.

7. See Luke 9:35; Joseph Smith—History 1:17.
8. See Alma 36:17–20.
9. See 2 Corinthians 5:17.
10. See Doctrine and Covenants 50:24.
11. 1 John 3:2.
12. See Mormon 7:7.
13. John 10:16.
14. Doctrine and Covenants 59:5.
15. See Doctrine and Covenants 88:62–63.
16. See Doctrine and Covenants 14:7; 41:5.
17. See Doctrine and Covenants 12:8; 59:6.
18. Doctrine and Covenants 121:45. The process of caring for others allows both rich and poor a way toward refining their characters and leads them both toward exaltation (see Doctrine and Covenants 104:15–18).
19. See Doctrine and Covenants 81:5.
20. 1 John 3:18.
21. What qualifies someone to preach the gospel? The Savior answers, "Whosoever will thrust in his sickle and reap, the same is called of God" (Doctrine and Covenants 11:4). Ultimately, it is our desires that qualify us for the work of proclaiming the word of God (see Doctrine and Covenants 4:3).
22. See Doctrine and Covenants 124:39.
23. Doctrine and Covenants 25:10.
24. See Mosiah 16:11.
25. See Doctrine and Covenants 82:9.
26. This was the question the multitude asked Jesus on the banks of the Sea of Galilee. It is a starting question for us as we contemplate becoming disciples of Jesus Christ. (See John 6:28.)
27. See Alma 41:4–5, 10–11.
28. See Doctrine and Covenants 88:63.
29. See Proverbs 3:5.
30. See 3 Nephi 9:20; Doctrine and Covenants 20:37.
31. See Doctrine and Covenants 88:63.

ESSENTIAL CONVERSATIONS

JOY D. JONES
Recently Released Primary General President

Have you ever wondered why we call Primary "Primary"? While the name refers to spiritual learning children receive in their earliest years, to me it is also a reminder of a powerful truth. To our Heavenly Father, children have *never* been secondary—they have *always* been "primary."[1]

He trusts us to value, respect, and protect them as children of God. That means we never harm them physically, verbally, or emotionally in any way, even when tensions and pressures run high. Instead we *value* children, and we do all we can to combat the evils of abuse. Their care is primary to us—as it is to Him.[2]

One young mother and father sat at their kitchen table reviewing their day. From down the hall, they heard a thud. The mother asked, "What was that?"

Then they heard a soft cry coming from their four-year-old son's bedroom. They rushed down the hall. There he was, lying on the floor next to his bed. The mother picked up the little boy and asked him what had happened.

He said, "I fell out of bed."

She said, "Why did you fall out of bed?"

He shrugged and said, "I don't know. I guess I just didn't get far enough in."

It is about this "getting far enough in" that I would like to speak this morning. It is our privilege and responsibility to help children "get far enough in" to the gospel of Jesus Christ. And we cannot begin too soon.

There is a uniquely special time in children's lives when they are protected from Satan's influence. It is a time when they are innocent and sin free.[3] It is a sacred time for parent and child. Children are to be taught, by word and example, before and after they have "arrived unto the years of accountability before God."[4]

President Henry B. Eyring taught: "We have the greatest

opportunity with the young. The best time to teach is early, while children are still immune to the temptations of [the] mortal enemy, and long before the words of truth may be harder for them to hear in the noise of their personal struggles."[5] Such teaching will help them realize their divine identity, their purpose, and the rich blessings that await them as they make sacred covenants and receive ordinances along the covenant path.

We cannot wait for conversion to simply happen to our children. Accidental conversion is *not* a principle of the gospel of Jesus Christ. Becoming like our Savior will not happen randomly. Being intentional in loving, teaching, and testifying can help children begin at a young age to feel the influence of the Holy Ghost. The Holy Ghost is essential to our children's testimony of and conversion to Jesus Christ; we desire them to "always remember him, that they may have his Spirit to be with them."[6]

Consider the value of family conversations about the gospel of Jesus Christ, *essential* conversations, that can invite the Spirit. When we have such conversations with our children, we help them create a foundation, "which is a sure foundation, a foundation whereon if [they] build they cannot fall."[7] When we strengthen a child, we strengthen the family.

These vital discussions can lead children to:

- Understand the doctrine of repentance.
- Have faith in Christ, the Son of the living God.
- Choose baptism and the gift of the Holy Ghost when eight years old.[8]
- And pray and "walk uprightly before the Lord."[9]

The Savior urged, "Therefore I give unto you a commandment, to teach these things *freely* unto your children."[10] And what did He want us to teach so freely?

1. The Fall of Adam
2. The Atonement of Jesus Christ
3. The importance of being born again[11]

Elder D. Todd Christofferson said, "Certainly the adversary is pleased when parents neglect to teach and train their children to have faith in Christ and be spiritually born again."[12]

In contrast, the Savior would have us help children "put [their] trust in that Spirit which leadeth to do good."[13] To do so, we can assist children in recognizing when they are feeling the Spirit and in discerning what actions cause the Spirit to leave. Thus they learn to repent and return to the light through the Atonement of Jesus Christ. This helps encourage spiritual resilience.

We can have fun helping our children build spiritual resilience at any age. It doesn't have to be complicated or time intensive. Simple, caring conversations can lead children to know not only *what* they believe, but most important, *why* they believe it. Caring conversations, happening naturally and consistently, can lead to better understanding and answers. Let's not allow the convenience of electronic devices to keep us from teaching and listening to our children and looking into their eyes.

Additional opportunities for essential conversations can occur through role-playing. Family members can act out situations of being tempted or pressured to make a bad choice. Such an exercise can fortify children to be prepared in a challenging setting. For example, we can act it out and then talk it out as we ask children what they would do:

- If they are tempted to break the Word of Wisdom.
- If they are exposed to pornography.
- If they are tempted to lie, steal, or cheat.
- If they hear something from a friend or teacher at school that disputes their beliefs or values.

As they act it out and then talk it out, rather than being caught unprepared in a hostile peer group setting, children can be armed with "the shield of faith wherewith [they] shall be able to quench *all* the fiery darts of the wicked."[14]

A close personal friend learned this crucial lesson as an 18-year-old. He enlisted in the United States military during the conflict between the United States and Vietnam. He was assigned to basic training in the infantry to become a foot soldier. He explained that the training was grueling. He described his drill instructor as cruel and inhumane.

One particular day his squad was dressed in full battle gear, hiking in sweltering heat. The drill instructor suddenly shouted orders to drop to the ground and not move. The instructor was watching for even the *slightest* motion. Any movement would result in serious consequences later on. The squad suffered for more than two hours in the heat with growing anger and resentment toward their leader.

Many months later our friend found himself leading his squad through the jungles of Vietnam. This was real, not just training. Shots began to ring from high in the surrounding trees. The entire squad immediately dropped to the ground.

What was the enemy looking for? Movement. Any motion at all would draw fire. My friend said that as he lay sweating and motionless on the jungle floor, waiting for dark for several long hours, his thoughts reflected back on basic training. He remembered his intense dislike for his drill instructor. Now he felt intense gratitude—for what he had taught him and how he had prepared him for this critical situation. The drill instructor had wisely equipped our friend and his squad with the ability to know what to do when the battle was raging. He had, in effect, saved our friend's life.

How can we do the same for our children spiritually? Long before they enter the battlefield of life, how can we more fully strive to teach, fortify, and prepare them?[15] How can we invite them to "get far enough in"? Wouldn't we rather have them "sweat" in the safe learning environment of the home than *bleed on the battlefields of life*?

As I look back, there were times when my husband and I felt like drill instructors in our earnestness to help our children live the gospel of Jesus Christ. The prophet Jacob seemed to voice these same feelings when he said: "I am desirous for the welfare of your souls. Yea, mine anxiety is great for you; and ye yourselves know that it ever has been."[16]

As children learn and progress, their beliefs will be challenged. But as they are properly equipped, they can grow in faith, courage, and confidence, even in the midst of strong opposition.

Alma taught us to "prepare the minds of [the] children."[17] We are preparing the rising generation to be the future defenders of the faith, to understand "that [they] are free to act for [themselves]—to choose the way of everlasting death or the way of eternal life."[18] Children deserve to understand this great truth: eternity is the wrong thing to be wrong about.

May our simple yet essential conversations with our children help them to "enjoy the *words* of eternal life" now so that they may enjoy "eternal life in the world to come, even immortal glory."[19]

As we nurture and prepare our children, we allow for their agency, we love them with all our heart, we teach them God's commandments and His gift of repentance, and we never, *ever*, give up on them. After all, isn't this the Lord's way with each of us?

Let us "press forward with a steadfastness in Christ," knowing that we can have "a perfect brightness of hope"[20] through our loving Savior.

I testify that He is always the answer. In the sacred name of Jesus Christ, amen.

Notes

1. See 3 Nephi 17:23–24.
2. See Michaelene P. Grassli, "Behold Your Little Ones," *Ensign*, Nov. 1992, 93: "To me, the word *behold* is significant. It implies more than just 'look and see.' When the Lord instructed the Nephites to *behold* their little ones, I believe he told them to give attention to their children, to contemplate them, to look beyond the present and see their eternal possibilities."

    See also Russell M. Nelson, "Listen to Learn," *Ensign*, May 1991, 22: "To rule children by force is the technique of Satan, not of the Savior. No, we don't own our children. Our parental privilege is to love them, to lead them, and to let them go."
3. See Doctrine and Covenants 29:46–47.
4. Doctrine and Covenants 20:71.
5. Henry B. Eyring, "The Power of Teaching Doctrine," *Ensign*, May 1999, 74; *Liahona*, July 1999, 87.
6. Doctrine and Covenants 20:79.
7. Helaman 5:12.
8. See Doctrine and Covenants 68:25; see also Articles of Faith 1:4.
9. Doctrine and Covenants 68:28.
10. Moses 6:58; emphasis added.
11. See Moses 6:59; see also Doctrine and Covenants 20:29–31.
12. D. Todd Christofferson, "Why Marriage, Why Family?," *Ensign* or *Liahona*, May 2015, 52.
13. See Doctrine and Covenants 11:12–13; see also Doctrine and Covenants 93.

14. Doctrine and Covenants 27:17; emphasis added; see also Marion G. Romney, "Home Teaching and Family Home Evening," *Improvement Era*, June 1969, 97: "Satan, our enemy, is making an all-out assault upon righteousness. His well-marshaled forces are legion. Our children and youth are the targets of his main thrust. They are everywhere subjected to wicked and vicious propaganda. Every place they turn, they are buffeted with evil, cunningly devised to deceive and to destroy every sacred thing and every righteous principle. . . . If our children are to be sufficiently strengthened to stand against this satanic onslaught, they must be taught and trained in the home, as the Lord has directed."

15. See Russell M. Nelson, "Children of the Covenant," *Ensign*, May 1995, 32:

"Years ago as a young medical student I saw many patients afflicted with diseases that are now preventable. Today it is possible to immunize individuals against conditions that once were disabling—even deadly. One medical method by which acquired immunity is conferred is inoculation. The term *inoculate* is fascinating. It comes from two Latin roots: *in*, meaning 'within'; and *oculus*, meaning 'an eye.' The verb *to inoculate*, therefore, literally means 'to put an eye within'—to monitor against harm.

"An affliction like polio can cripple or destroy the body. An affliction like sin can cripple or destroy the spirit. The ravages of polio can now be prevented by immunization, but the ravages of sin require other means of prevention. Doctors cannot immunize against iniquity. Spiritual protection comes only from the Lord—and in his own way. Jesus chooses not to inoculate, but to indoctrinate. His method employs no vaccine; it utilizes the teaching of divine doctrine—a governing 'eye within'—to protect the eternal spirits of his children."

16. 2 Nephi 6:3.

17. Alma 39:16.

18. 2 Nephi 10:23.

19. Moses 6:59; emphasis added.

20. 2 Nephi 31:20.

TEACHING IN THE SAVIOR'S WAY

JAN E. NEWMAN

Second Counselor in the Sunday School General Presidency

Exceptional Teachers

A few months ago, a former classmate from my hometown of Overton, Nevada, suggested we put together a Christmas gift for our beloved kindergarten teacher, who had recently celebrated her 98th birthday. She taught us to be kind, the importance of a good nap, the joy of milk and graham crackers, and to love one another. Thank you, Sister Davis, for being such a wonderful teacher.

I had another exceptional teacher while attending Ricks College many years ago. I was preparing to serve a mission and thought it would be helpful to attend a missionary preparation class. What I experienced changed my life.

From the first day of class, I realized I was in the presence of a master teacher. The teacher was Brother F. Melvin Hammond. I knew Brother Hammond loved the Lord and he loved me. I could see it in his face and hear it in his voice. When he taught, the Spirit enlightened my mind. He taught doctrine, but he also invited me to learn it on my own. That invitation helped me clearly see my responsibility to learn the Lord's doctrine for myself. That experience changed me forever. Thank you, Brother Hammond, for teaching in the Savior's way.

Brothers and sisters, everyone deserves to have this kind of learning experience both at home and at church.

The introduction to *Come, Follow Me* gives a vision of what Christlike teaching can accomplish. "The aim of all gospel learning and teaching," it says, "is to deepen our conversion to Jesus Christ and help us become more like Him. . . . The kind of gospel learning that strengthens our faith and leads to the miracle of conversion doesn't happen all at once. It extends beyond [the] classroom into an individual's heart and home."[1]

The scriptures indicate that the Savior's ministry in ancient

America was so impactful and widespread that "the people were all converted unto the Lord, upon all the face of the land, both Nephites and Lamanites, and there were no contentions and disputations among them, and every man did deal justly one with another."[2]

How can our teaching have a similar effect on those we love? How can we teach more like the Savior and help others become more deeply converted? Allow me to offer a few suggestions.

Emulate the Savior

First and foremost, take it upon yourself to learn all you can about the Master Teacher Himself. How did He show love for others? What did they feel when He taught? What did He teach? What were His expectations of those He taught? After you explore questions like these, evaluate and adjust your way of teaching to be more like His.

The Church provides many teaching resources in the Gospel Library app and on ChurchofJesusChrist.org. One such resource is titled *Teaching in the Savior's Way*. I invite you to read and study its every word. Its principles will assist you in your efforts to be more Christlike in your teaching.

Unleash the Power of Families

My next suggestion can be illustrated with an experience I had a few months ago when I stopped by to visit a dear friend. I could hear his wife in the background speaking with someone, so I quickly excused myself so he could get back to his family.

An hour or so later I received this text message from his sweet wife: "Brother Newman, thanks for coming over. We should have invited you in, but I want to share with you what we were doing. Since the pandemic we have been discussing *Come, Follow Me* with our adult children every Sunday over Zoom. It has literally been working miracles. I think it is the first time our daughter has read the Book of Mormon on her own. Today was the last lesson on the Book of Mormon, and we were just finishing when you came by. . . .

I thought you would be interested to hear how *Come, Follow Me*, Zoom, and a pandemic have provided the opportunity at the right time to change a heart. . . . It makes me wonder how many little miracles have been taking place during this odd time."

This sounds to me like a fulfillment of the promise President Russell M. Nelson made in October 2018. He said that home-centered, Church-supported gospel learning "has the potential to unleash the power of families, as each family follows through conscientiously and carefully to transform their home into a sanctuary of faith. I promise that as you diligently work to remodel your home into a center of gospel learning, over time *your* Sabbath days will truly be a delight. *Your* children will be excited to learn and to live the Savior's teachings. . . . Changes in your family will be dramatic and sustaining."[3] What a beautiful promise!

To be truly life-changing, conversion to Jesus Christ must involve our whole soul and permeate every aspect of our lives. This is why it must be focused at the center of our lives—our families and homes.

Remember That Conversion Is Personal

My final suggestion is to remember that conversion must come from within. As illustrated in the parable of the ten virgins, we cannot give someone else the oil of our conversion, as much as we might want to. As Elder David A. Bednar taught: "This precious oil is acquired one drop at a time . . . patiently and persistently. No shortcut is available; no last-minute flurry of preparation is possible."[4]

Come, Follow Me is based on that truth. I compare it to the angel who helped Nephi learn about Jesus Christ by saying, "Look!"[5] Like that angel, *Come, Follow Me* invites us to look in the scriptures and the words of the modern-day prophets in order to find the Savior and hear Him. Like Nephi, we will be personally tutored by the Spirit while reading and pondering the word of God. *Come, Follow Me* is the springboard that helps each of us to dive deeply into the living waters of the doctrine of Christ.

A parent's responsibility is similar in many ways. Children

inherit many things from their parents, but a testimony is not one of them. We can't give our children a testimony any more than we can make a seed grow. But we can provide a nourishing environment, with good soil, free of thorns that would "choke the word." We can strive to create the ideal conditions so that our children—and others we love—can find place for the seed, "[hear] the word, and [understand] it"[6] and discover for themselves "that the seed is good."[7]

Several years ago, my son Jack and I had the opportunity to play the Old Course at St. Andrews in Scotland, where the game of golf began. It was simply amazing! Upon my return I tried to convey to others the magnitude of the experience. But I couldn't. Photos, videos, and my best descriptions were totally inadequate. I finally realized the only way for someone to know the grandeur of St. Andrews is to experience it—to see the vast fairways, breathe the air, feel the wind in their face, and hit a few errant shots into the cavernous bunkers and burly gorse bushes, which we did with great efficiency.

So it is with the word of God. We can teach it, we can preach it, we can explain it. We can talk about it, we can describe it, we can even testify of it. But until a person feels the sacred word of God distill upon his or her soul like the dews from heaven through the power of the Spirit,[8] it will be like looking at a postcard or someone else's vacation photos. You have to go there yourself. Conversion is a personal journey—a journey of gathering.

Everyone who teaches in the home and at church can offer to others the opportunity to have their own spiritual experiences. Through these experiences, they will come to "know the truth of all things" for themselves.[9] President Nelson taught, "If you have sincere questions about the gospel or the Church, as you choose to let God prevail, you will be led to find and understand the absolute, eternal truths that will guide your life and help you stay firmly on the covenant path."[10]

Dramatically Improve Teaching

I invite leaders and teachers in every organization of the Church to counsel together with parents and youth in order to dramatically improve teaching at every level—in stakes, in wards, and in homes. This will be achieved by teaching the doctrine and inviting Spirit-filled discussion about the truths the Holy Ghost has taught us in the quiet moments of our personal study.

My dear friends in Christ, the responsibility rests squarely upon each of us to follow the example of the Master and teach like Him. His way is the true way! As we follow Him "when he shall appear we shall be like him, for we shall see him as he is; that we may have this hope; that we may be purified even as he is pure."[11] In the name of He who is risen, the Master Teacher Himself, Jesus Christ, amen.

Notes

1. *Come, Follow Me—For Individuals and Families: Doctrine and Covenants 2021*, vi.
2. 4 Nephi 1:2.
3. Russell M. Nelson, "Becoming Exemplary Latter-day Saints," *Ensign* or *Liahona*, Nov. 2018, 113.
4. David A. Bednar, "Converted unto the Lord," *Ensign* or *Liahona*, Nov. 2012, 109.
5. See 1 Nephi 11:8–36.
6. Matthew 13:18–23.
7. Alma 32:30.
8. See Doctrine and Covenants 121:45.
9. Moroni 10:5.
10. Russell M. Nelson, "Let God Prevail," *Ensign* or *Liahona*, Nov. 2020, 94.
11. Moroni 7:48.

HEARTS KNIT TOGETHER

ELDER GARY E. STEVENSON

Of the Quorum of the Twelve Apostles

Introduction

Isn't it fascinating that significant scientific discoveries are sometimes inspired by events as simple as an apple falling from a tree?

Today, let me share a discovery that happened because of a sample group of rabbits.

In the 1970s, researchers set up an experiment to examine the effects of diet on heart health. Over several months, they fed a control group of rabbits a high-fat diet and monitored their blood pressure, heart rate, and cholesterol.

As expected, many of the rabbits showed a buildup of fatty deposits on the inside of their arteries. Yet this was not all! Researchers had discovered something that made little sense. Although all of the rabbits had a buildup, one group surprisingly had as much as 60 percent less than the others. It appeared as though they were looking at two different groups of rabbits.

To scientists, results like this can cause lost sleep. How could this be? The rabbits were all the same breed from New Zealand, from a virtually identical gene pool. They each received equal amounts of the same food.

What could this mean?

Did the results invalidate the study? Were there flaws in the experiment design?

The scientists struggled to understand this unexpected outcome!

Eventually, they turned their attention to the research staff. Was it possible that researchers had done something to influence the results? As they pursued this, they discovered that every rabbit with fewer fatty deposits had been under the care of one researcher. She fed the rabbits the same food as everyone else. But, as one scientist reported, "she was an unusually kind and caring individual."

When she fed the rabbits, "she talked to them, cuddled and petted them. . . . 'She couldn't help it. It's just how she was.'"[1]

She did more than simply give the rabbits food. She gave them love!

At first glance, it seemed unlikely that this could be the reason for the dramatic difference, but the research team could see no other possibility.

So they repeated the experiment—this time tightly controlling for every other variable. When they analyzed the results, the same thing happened! The rabbits under the care of the loving researcher had significantly higher health outcomes.

The scientists published the results of this study in the prestigious journal *Science*.[2]

Years later the findings of this experiment still seem influential in the medical community. In recent years, Dr. Kelli Harding published a book titled *The Rabbit Effect* that takes its name from the experiment. Her conclusion: "Take a rabbit with an unhealthy lifestyle. Talk to it. Hold it. Give it affection. . . . The relationship made a difference. . . . Ultimately," she concludes, "what affects our health in the most meaningful ways has as much to do with how we treat one another, how we live, and how we think about what it means to be human."[3]

In a secular world, bridges connecting science with gospel truths sometimes seem few and far between. Yet as Christians, followers of Jesus Christ, Latter-day Saints, the results of this scientific study may seem more intuitive than astonishing. For me, this lays another brick in the foundation of kindness as a fundamental, healing gospel principle—one that can heal hearts emotionally, spiritually, and, as demonstrated here, even physically.

Hearts Knit Together

When asked, "Master, which is the great commandment?" the Savior replied to "love the Lord thy God with all thy heart," followed by, "Thou shalt love thy neighbour as thyself."[4] The Savior's response reinforces our heavenly duty. An ancient prophet commanded "that there should be no contention one with another, but that [we] should look forward . . . , having [our] *hearts knit together* in unity and in love one towards another."[5] We are further taught that "power or influence . . . ought to be maintained . . . by gentleness and meekness, . . . by kindness, . . . without guile."[6]

I believe this principle has a universal application to all Latter-day Saints: adults, youth, and children.

With that in mind, let me speak directly to you who are Primary-age children for a moment.

You already understand how important it is to be kind. The chorus of one of your Primary songs, "I'm Trying to Be like Jesus," teaches:

> *Love one another as Jesus loves you.*
> *Try to show kindness in all that you do.*
> *Be gentle and loving in deed and in thought,*
> *For these are the things Jesus taught.*[7]

Even still, you may sometimes have a hard time. Here is a story that might help you about a Primary boy named Minchan Kim from South Korea. His family joined the Church about six years ago.

"One day at school, a few of my classmates were making fun of another student by calling him names. It looked like fun, so for a few weeks I joined in with them.

"Several weeks later, the boy told me even though he pretended he didn't care, he was hurt by our words, and he cried every night. I almost cried when he told me. I felt very sorry and wanted to help him. The next day I went up to him and put my arm around his shoulder and apologized, saying, 'I'm really sorry that I made fun of you.' He nodded at my words, and his eyes filled up with tears.

"But the other kids were still making fun of him. Then I remembered what I learned in Primary class: choose the right. So I asked my classmates to stop. Most of them decided not to change, and they were mad at me. But one of the other boys said he was sorry, and the three of us became good friends.

"Even though a few people still made fun of him, he felt better because he had us.

"I chose the right by helping a friend in need."[8]

Isn't this a good example for you to try to become like Jesus?

Now, for young men and young women, as you grow older, making fun of others can evolve very dangerously. Anxiety, depression, and worse are often the companions of bullying. "While bullying is not a new concept, social media and technology have brought bullying to a new level. It becomes a more constant, ever-present threat—cyberbullying."[9]

Clearly, the adversary is using this to hurt your generation. There is no place for this in your cyberspace, neighborhoods, schools, quorums, or classes. Please do all you can to make these places kinder and safer. If you passively observe or participate in any of this, I know of no better advice than that previously given by Elder Dieter F. Uchtdorf:

"When it comes to hating, gossiping, ignoring, ridiculing, holding grudges, or wanting to cause harm, please apply the following:

"Stop it!"[10]

Did you hear that? Stop it! As you extend yourself with kindness, care, and compassion, even digitally, I promise that you will lift up arms that hang down and will heal hearts.

Having spoken to Primary children and youth, I now direct my remarks to adults of the Church. We have a primary responsibility to set a tone and be role models of kindness, inclusion, and civility—to teach Christlike behavior to the rising generation in what we say and how we act. It is especially important as we observe a marked societal shift toward division in politics, social class, and nearly every other man-made distinction.

President M. Russell Ballard has also taught that Latter-day Saints must be kind not only to each other but also to everyone around us. He observed: "Occasionally I hear of members offending those of other faiths by overlooking them and leaving them out. This can occur especially in communities where our members are the majority. I have heard about narrow-minded parents who tell children that they cannot play with a particular child in the neighborhood simply because his or her family does not belong to our Church. This kind of behavior is not in keeping with the teachings of the Lord Jesus Christ. I cannot comprehend why any member of our Church would allow these kinds of things to happen. . . . I have never heard the members of this Church urged to be anything but loving, kind, tolerant, and benevolent to our friends and neighbors of other faiths."[11]

The Lord expects us to teach that inclusion is a positive means toward unity and that exclusion leads to division.

As followers of Jesus Christ, we are dismayed when we hear of how children of God are mistreated based on their race. We have been heartbroken to hear of recent attacks on people who are Black, Asian, Latino, or of any other group. Prejudice, racial tension, or violence should never have any place in our neighborhoods, communities, or within the Church.

Let each of us, no matter our age, strive to be our best.

Love Your Enemy

As you strive to extend yourself in love, respect, and kindness, you will undoubtedly be hurt or negatively affected by the bad choices of others. What do we do then? We follow the Lord's admonition to "love your enemies . . . and pray for them which despitefully use you."[12]

We do all we can to overcome the adversity that is placed in our path. We strive to endure to the end, all the time praying that the hand of the Lord will change our circumstances. We offer thanksgiving for those He places in our path to assist us.

I am moved by an example of this from our early Church history. During the winter of 1838, Joseph Smith and other Church leaders were detained in Liberty Jail when the Latter-day Saints were forcibly driven from their homes in the state of Missouri. The Saints were destitute, friendless, and suffering greatly from the cold and lack of resources. The residents of Quincy, Illinois, saw their desperate plight and reached out in compassion and friendship.

Wandle Mace, a resident of Quincy, later recalled when he first saw the Saints along the Mississippi River in makeshift tents: "Some had sheets stretched, to make a little shelter from the wind, . . . the children were shivering around a fire which the wind blew about so it done them very little good. The poor Saints were suffering terribly."[13]

Seeing the plight of the Saints, Quincy residents rallied together to provide aid, some even assisting in transporting their new friends across the river. Mace continued: "[They] donated liberally; the merchants vying with each other as to which could be the most liberal . . . with . . . pork, . . . sugar, . . . shoes and clothing, everything these poor outcasts so much needed."[14] Before long, the refugees outnumbered the Quincy residents, who opened their homes and shared their meager resources at great personal sacrifice.[15]

Many Saints survived the harsh winter only because of the compassion and generosity of the residents of Quincy. These earthly angels opened their hearts and homes, bringing lifesaving nourishment, warmth, and—perhaps most importantly—a hand of friendship to the suffering Saints. Although their stay in Quincy was relatively short, the Saints never forgot their debt of gratitude toward their beloved neighbors, and Quincy became known as the "city of refuge."[16]

When adversity and affliction are brought upon us by critical, negative, even mean-spirited acts, we can choose to hope in Christ. This hope comes from His invitation and promise to "be of good cheer, for I will lead you along"[17] and that He will consecrate your afflictions for your gain.[18]

The Good Shepherd

Let us conclude where we began: a compassionate caregiver, extending herself in kindness with a nurturing spirit, and an unexpected outcome—healing the hearts of animals over whom she had stewardship. Why? Because it was just how she was!

As we look through a gospel lens, we recognize that we too are under the watchcare of a compassionate caregiver, who extends

Himself in kindness and a nurturing spirit. The Good Shepherd knows each one of us by name and has a personal interest in us.[19] The Lord Jesus Christ Himself said: "I am the good shepherd, and know my sheep. . . . And I [will] lay down my life for the sheep."[20]

On this holy Easter weekend, I find abiding peace in knowing that "the Lord is my shepherd"[21] and that each of us is known by Him and under His kind watchcare. When we confront life's wind and rainstorms, sickness and injuries, the Lord—our Shepherd, our Caregiver—will nourish us with love and kindness. He will heal our hearts and restore our souls.

Of this I testify—and of Jesus Christ as our Savior and our Redeemer—in the name of Jesus Christ, amen.

Notes

1. See Kelli Harding, *The Rabbit Effect* (2019), xxiii–xxiv.
2. See Robert M. Nerem, Murina J. Levesque, and J. Frederick Cornhill, "Social Environment as a Factor in Diet-Induced Atherosclerosis," *Science*, vol. 208, no. 4451 (June 27, 1980), 1475–76.
3. Harding, *The Rabbit Effect*, xxiv, xxv.
4. See Matthew 22:36–39.
5. Mosiah 18:21; emphasis added.
6. Doctrine and Covenants 121:41–42.
7. "I'm Trying to Be like Jesus," *Children's Songbook*, 79.
8. Adapted from Minchan K., "The Apology," *Friend*, Jan. 2020, 35.
9. Frances Dalomba, "Social Media: The Good, the Bad, and the Ugly," Lifespan, lifespan.org.
10. Dieter F. Uchtdorf, "The Merciful Obtain Mercy," *Ensign* or *Liahona*, May 2012, 75.
11. M. Russell Ballard, "Doctrine of Inclusion," *Ensign*, Nov. 2001, 36–37; *Liahona*, Jan. 2002, 41.
12. Luke 6:27–28.
13. Wandle Mace autobiography, circa 1890, typescript, 32–33, Church History Library, Salt Lake City.
14. Wandle Mace autobiography, 33; spelling and capitalization standardized.
15. See Richard E. Bennett, "'Quincy—the Home of Our Adoption': A Study of the Mormons in Quincy, Illinois, 1838–40," *Mormon Historical Studies*, vol. 2, no. 1 (Spring 2001), 110–11.
16. See Susan Easton Black, "Quincy–A City of Refuge," *Mormon Historical Studies*, vol. 2, no. 1 (Spring 2001), 83–94.
17. Doctrine and Covenants 78:18.
18. See 2 Nephi 2:2.
19. See James E. Talmage, *Jesus the Christ* (1916), 417.
20. John 10:14, 15.
21. Psalm 23:1.

ROOM IN THE INN

ELDER GERRIT W. GONG
Of the Quorum of the Twelve Apostles

Dear brothers and sisters, although he passed away 20 years ago, there are times I miss my father. Easter promises I will see him again.

When I was in graduate school in England, my father came to visit. His father's heart knew I missed home.

My father loved adventure except in food. Even in France, noted for its cuisine, he would say, "Let's eat Chinese food." A long-serving patriarch in the Church, my father was spiritual and compassionate. One night, as emergency vehicles with loud sirens raced through Paris, he said, "Gerrit, those cries are the wounds of a city."

On that trip, I felt other cries and wounds. A young woman was selling ice cream from a small pushcart. Her wafer cones were just the size for a single scoop of ice cream. For some reason, a large man confronted the young woman. Yelling and pushing, he tipped over her cart, spilling her ice-cream cones. There was nothing I could do as he crushed the cones with his boots. I can still see the young woman on her knees in the street, trying to save broken wafer pieces, tears of anguish streaming down her face. Her image haunts me, a reminder of the unkindness, uncaring, misunderstanding we too often inflict on each other.

On another afternoon, near Paris, my father and I visited the great cathedral at Chartres. Malcolm Miller,[1] a world expert on the cathedral, pointed out three sets of Chartres stained-glass windows. He said they tell a story.

The first windows show Adam and Eve leaving the Garden of Eden.

The second recount the parable of the good Samaritan.

The third depict the Lord's Second Coming.

Taken together, these stained-glass windows can describe our eternal journey. They invite us to welcome all with room in His inn.[2]

Like Adam and Eve, we come into a world of thorns and thistles.[3]

On our dusty roads to Jericho, we are beset upon, wounded, and left in pain.[4]

Though we should help each other, too often we pass to the other side of the road, for whatever reason.

However, with compassion, the Good Samaritan stops and binds our wounds with wine and oil. Symbols of the sacrament and other ordinances, the wine and oil point us to the spiritual healing in Jesus Christ.[5] The Good Samaritan puts us on His own donkey or, in some stained-glass accounts, carries us on His shoulders. He brings us to the inn, which can represent His Church. At the Inn, the Good Samaritan says, "Take care of him; . . . when I come again, I will repay thee."[6] The Good Samaritan, a symbol of our Savior, promises to return, this time in majesty and glory.

In this Easter season, Jesus Christ invites us to become, like Him, a good Samaritan, to make His Inn (His Church) a refuge for all from life's bruises and storms.[7] We prepare for His promised Second Coming as each day we do unto "the least of these"[8] as we would unto Him. "The least of these" is each of us.

As we come with the Good Samaritan to the Inn, we learn five things about Jesus Christ and ourselves.

First, we come to the Inn as we are, with the foibles and imperfections we each have. Yet we all have something needed to contribute. Our journey to God is often found together. We belong as united community—whether confronting pandemics, storms, wildfires, droughts or quietly meeting daily needs. We receive inspiration as we counsel together, listening to each person, including each sister, and the Spirit.

As our hearts change and we receive His image in our countenance,[9] we see Him and ourselves in His Church. In Him, we find clarity, not dissonance. In Him, we find cause to do good, reason to be good, and increasing capacity to become better. In Him, we discover abiding faith, liberating selflessness, caring change, and trust in God. In His Inn, we find and deepen our personal relationship with God, our Father, and Jesus Christ.

He trusts us to help make the Inn the place He needs it to

be. As we offer our talents and best efforts, His spiritual gifts also strengthen and bless.[10]

A Spanish language interpreter told me, "Elder Gong, I knew by the Spirit what you were going to say so I could translate," this faithful brother said, "by the gift of tongues."

Gifts of faith and assurance come, manifest differently in different situations. One dear sister received spiritual comfort as her husband passed away from COVID-19. She said, "I know my dear husband and I will be together again." In a different COVID situation, another dear sister said, "I felt I should plead with the Lord and the doctors to give my husband just a little more time."

Second, He entreats us to make His Inn a place of grace and space, where each can gather, with room for all. As disciples of Jesus Christ, all are equal, with no second-class groups.

All are welcome to attend sacrament meetings, other Sunday meetings, and social events.[11] We reverently worship our Savior, thoughtful and considerate of each other. We see and acknowledge each person. We smile, sit with those sitting alone, learn names, including of new converts, returning brothers and sisters, young women and young men, each dear Primary child.

Imagining ourselves in their place, we welcome friends, visitors, new move-ins, busy individuals pulled in too many directions. We mourn, rejoice, and are there for each other. When we fall short of our ideals and are rushed, unaware, judgmental, or prejudiced, we seek each other's forgiveness and do better.

A family from Africa now living in the United States said, "From the first day, Church members were friendly and welcoming. Everyone made us feel at home. No one looked down on us." The father said, "The Holy Bible teaches gospel fruits come from gospel roots." "And the missionaries," the father and mother said, "we want our son and daughter to grow up like those missionaries." Brothers and sisters, may we each warmly welcome all to His Inn.

Third, in His Inn we learn perfection is in Jesus Christ, not in the perfectionism of the world. Unreal and unrealistic, the world's "insta-perfect" filtered perfectionism can make us feel inadequate,

31

captive to swipes, likes, or double taps. In contrast, our Savior, Jesus Christ, knows everything about us we don't want anyone else to know, and He still loves us. His is a gospel of second and third chances, made possible by His atoning sacrifice.[12] He invites each of us to be a good Samaritan, less judgmental and more forgiving of ourselves and of each other, even as we strive more fully to keep His commandments.

We help ourselves as we help each other. A family I know lived near a busy road. Travelers often stopped to ask for help. Early one morning the family heard loud pounding on their door. Tired and worried who it would be at 2:00 a.m., they wondered if, just this once, someone else could help. As the insistent knocking continued, they heard, "Fire—there's a fire in the back of your house!" Good Samaritans help each other.

Fourth, at His Inn we become part of a gospel community centered in Jesus Christ, anchored in restored truth, living prophets and apostles, and another testament of Jesus Christ—the Book of Mormon. He brings us to His Inn and also to His house—the holy temple. The house of the Lord is a place where, as with the wounded man on the road to Jericho, the Good Samaritan can cleanse and clothe us, prepare us to return to God's presence, and unite us eternally in God's family. His temples are open to all who live His gospel with faith and obedience.

Temple rejoicing includes gospel unity amidst diverse heritages, cultures, languages, and generations. At the groundbreaking for the Taylorsville Utah Temple, 17-year-old Max Harker shared a legacy of family faith begun six generations earlier by his great-great-great-grandfather Joseph Harker and his wife, Susannah Sneath. In the restored gospel of Jesus Christ, we can each become a strong link in our family generations.

Finally, fifth, we rejoice that God loves His children in our different backgrounds and circumstances, in every nation, kindred, and tongue, with room for all in His Inn.

Over the past 40 years, Church members have become increasingly international. Since 1998, more Church members have lived outside than inside the United States and Canada. By 2025, we anticipate as many Church members may live in Latin America as in the United States and Canada. The gathering of Father Lehi's faithful descendants is fulfilling prophecy. Faithful Saints, including in the pioneer corridor, remain a reservoir of devotion and service for the worldwide Church.

Also, the majority of adult Church members are now unmarried, widowed, or divorced. This is a significant change. It includes more than half our Relief Society sisters and more than half our adult priesthood brothers. This demographic pattern has been the case in the worldwide Church since 1992 and in the Church in the United States and Canada since 2019.

Our standing before the Lord and in His Church is not a matter of our marital status but of our becoming faithful and valiant disciples of Jesus Christ.[13] Adults want to be seen as adults and to be responsible and contribute as adults. Disciples of Jesus Christ come from everywhere, in every shape, size, hue, and age, each with talents, righteous desires, and immense capacities to bless and serve. We seek daily to follow Jesus Christ with faith unto repentance[14] and enduring joy.

During this life, we sometimes wait upon the Lord. We may not yet be where we hope and wish to be in the future. A devout sister says, "Waiting faithfully upon the Lord for His blessings is a holy position. It must not be met with pity, patronizing, or judgment but instead with sacred honor."[15] In the meantime, we live now, not waiting for life to begin.

Isaiah promises, "They that wait upon the Lord shall renew their strength; they shall mount up with wings as eagles; they shall run, and not be weary; and they shall walk, and not faint."[16]

Our Good Samaritan promises to return. Miracles occur when we care for each other as He would. When we come with broken hearts and contrite spirits,[17] we can find voice in Jesus Christ and be encircled in His understanding arms of safety.[18] Sacred ordinances offer covenant belonging and "the power of godliness"[19] to sanctify inner intent and outward action. With His loving-kindness and long-suffering, His Church becomes our Inn.

As we create room in His Inn, welcoming all, our Good Samaritan can heal us on our dusty mortal roads. With perfect love, our Father and His Son, Jesus Christ, promise "peace in this world, and eternal life in the world to come"[20]—"that where I am ye shall be also."[21] I so gratefully witness and testify in the sacred and holy name of Jesus Christ, amen.

Notes

1. Malcolm Miller has lectured at Chartres Cathedral and around the world for over 60 years.
2. See Luke 10:34; in contrast, see Luke 2:7.
3. See Genesis 3:18.
4. See the parable of the good Samaritan in Luke 10:30–37.
5. See Hugh Nibley, *Since Cumorah*, 2nd ed., vol. 7 of *The Collected Works of Hugh Nibley* (1988), 100, in John W. Welch, "The Good Samaritan: A Type and Shadow of the Plan of Salvation," *BYU Studies*, vol. 38, no. 2 (1999), 54.
6. Luke 10:35.
7. See Doctrine and Covenants 115:6.
8. Matthew 25:40.
9. See Alma 5:14.
10. See Moroni 10:8–18; Doctrine and Covenants 46:11–26.
11. See *General Handbook: Serving in The Church of Jesus Christ of Latter-day Saints*, 38.1.1, ChurchofJesusChrist.org.
12. See Alma 34:14–16.
13. See Doctrine and Covenants 138:12: "faithful in the testimony of Jesus"; see also Doctrine and Covenants 76:79.
14. See Alma 34:16–17.
15. Personal conversation, used by permission.
16. Isaiah 40:31.
17. See 2 Nephi 2:7; 3 Nephi 9:20; Doctrine and Covenants 59:8.
18. See Alma 34:16.
19. Doctrine and Covenants 84:20.
20. Doctrine and Covenants 59:23.
21. Doctrine and Covenants 132:23.

I LOVE TO SEE THE TEMPLE

PRESIDENT HENRY B. EYRING
Second Counselor in the First Presidency

My dear brothers and sisters, I am grateful to be with you in this first session of general conference. The speakers, the music, and the prayer have brought the Spirit—as well as a feeling of light and hope.

That feeling has brought back to my memory the first day I walked into the Salt Lake Temple. I was a young man. My parents were my only companions that day. Inside, they paused for a moment to be greeted by a temple worker. I walked on ahead of them, alone for a moment.

I was greeted by a little white-haired lady in a beautiful white temple dress. She looked up at me and smiled and then said very softly, "Welcome to the temple, Brother Eyring." I thought for a moment she was an angel because she knew my name. I had not realized that a small card with my name on it had been placed on the lapel of my suit coat.

I stepped past her and stopped. I looked up at a high white ceiling that made the room so light it seemed almost as if it were open to the sky. And in that moment, the thought came into my mind in these clear words: "I have been in this lighted place before." But then immediately there came into my mind, not in my own voice, these words: "No, you have never been here before. You are remembering a moment before you were born. You were in a sacred place like this."

On the outside of our temples, we place the words "Holiness to the Lord." I know for myself that those words are true. The temple is a holy place where *revelation* comes to us easily if our hearts are open to it and we are worthy of it.

Later that first day I again felt the same Spirit. The temple ceremony includes some words that brought a feeling of burning in my heart, confirming that what was being portrayed was true. What I felt was personal to me regarding my future, and it became a reality 40 years later through a call to serve from the Lord.

I experienced the same feeling when I was married in the Logan Utah Temple. President Spencer W. Kimball performed the sealing. In the few words he spoke, he gave this counsel: "Hal and Kathy, live so that when the call comes, you can walk away easily."

As he said those few words, I saw clearly in my mind, in full color, a steep hill and a road leading up to the top. A white fence ran on the left side of the road and disappeared into a row of trees at the top of the hill. A white house was barely visible through the trees.

One year later, I recognized that hill as my father-in-law drove us up that road. It was in detail what I saw when President Kimball gave his counsel in the temple.

When we got to the top of the hill, my father-in-law stopped by the white house. He told us that he and his wife were buying the property and that he wanted his daughter and me to live in the guesthouse. They would live in the main house, just a few feet away. So, during the 10 years we lived in that lovely family setting, my wife and I would say almost every day, "We had better enjoy this because we aren't going to be here long."

A call came from the Church commissioner of education, Neal A. Maxwell. The warning given by President Kimball to be able to "walk away easily" became a reality. It was a call to leave what seemed an idyllic family situation to serve in an assignment in a place that I knew nothing about. Our family was ready to leave that blessed time and place because a prophet, in a holy temple, a place of revelation, saw a future event for which we then were prepared.

I know that temples of the Lord are holy places. My purpose today in speaking of temples is to increase your desire and mine to be worthy and ready for the increased opportunities for temple experiences that are coming for us.

For me, the greatest motivation to be worthy of temple experiences is what the Lord has said of His holy houses:

"Inasmuch as my people build a house unto me in the name of

the Lord, and do not suffer any unclean thing to come into it, that it be not defiled, my glory shall rest upon it;

"Yea, and my presence shall be there, for I will come into it, and all the pure in heart that shall come into it shall see God.

"But if it be defiled I will not come into it, and my glory shall not be there; for I will not come into unholy temples."[1]

President Russell M. Nelson made clear for us that we can "see" the Savior in the temple in the sense that He becomes no longer unknown to us. President Nelson said this: "We understand Him. We comprehend His work and His glory. And we begin to feel the infinite impact of His matchless life."[2]

If you or I should go to the temple insufficiently pure, we would not be able to see, by the power of the Holy Ghost, the spiritual teaching about the Savior that we can receive in the temple.

When we are worthy to receive such teaching, there can grow through our temple experience hope, joy, and optimism throughout our lives. That hope, joy, and optimism are available only through accepting the ordinances performed in holy temples. It is in the temple that we can receive the assurance of loving family connections that will continue after death and last for eternity.

Years ago, while I was serving as a bishop, a handsome young man resisted my invitation to become worthy to live with God in families forever. In a belligerent way he told me of the good times he had with his friends. I let him talk. Then he told me about a moment during one of his parties, in the midst of the raucous noise, when he suddenly realized that he felt lonely. I asked him what had happened. He said that he had remembered a time as a little boy, sitting on his mother's lap, with her arms around him. For that moment while he told that story, he teared up. I said to him what I know is true: "The only way you can have the feeling of that family embrace forever is to become worthy yourself and help others to receive the sealing ordinances of the temple."

We don't know the details of family connections in the spirit world or what may come after we are resurrected. But we do know that the prophet Elijah came as promised to turn the hearts of the fathers to the children and the children to the fathers.[3] And we know that our eternal happiness depends on our doing our best to offer the same lasting happiness to as many of our kindred as we can.

I feel the same desire to succeed in inviting living family members to desire to become worthy to receive and to honor the sealing ordinances of the temple. That is part of the promised gathering of Israel in the last days on both sides of the veil.

One of our greatest opportunities is when our family members are young. They are born with the Light of Christ as a gift. It enables them to sense what is good and what is evil. For that reason, even seeing a temple or a picture of a temple can cultivate in a child a desire to be worthy and privileged someday to go inside.

The day can then come when, as a youth, they receive a temple recommend to perform proxy baptisms in the temple. In that experience, their feeling can grow that the ordinances of the temple always point to the Savior and His Atonement. As they feel they are offering a person in the spirit world the chance to be cleansed of sin, their feeling will grow of helping the Savior in His sacred work of blessing a child of our Heavenly Father.

I have seen the power of that experience change the life of a young person. Years ago I went with a daughter to a temple in the late afternoon. She was the last to serve as proxy in the baptistry. My daughter was asked if she could stay longer to complete the ordinances for all of the people whose names were prepared. She said yes.

I watched as my little daughter stepped into the baptismal font. The baptisms began. My little daughter had water streaming down her face each time she was lifted out of the water. She was asked again and again, "Can you do more?" Each time she said yes.

As a concerned father, I began to hope that she might be excused from doing more. But I remember still her firmness when she was asked if she could do more and she said in a determined little voice, "Yes." She stayed until the last person on the list that day had received the blessing of baptism in the name of Jesus Christ.

When I walked out of the temple with her that night, I

wondered at what I had seen. A child had been lifted and changed before my eyes by serving the Lord in His house. I still remember the feeling of light and peace as we walked together from the temple.

Years have passed. She is still saying yes to the question from the Lord if she will do more for Him when it is very hard. That is what temple service can do to change and lift us. That is why my hope for you and for all your beloved family is that you will grow in desire and determination to be worthy to go into the house of the Lord as often as your circumstances allow.

He wants to welcome you there. I pray that you will try to build desire in the hearts of Heavenly Father's children to go there, where they can feel close to Him, and that you will also invite your ancestors to qualify to be with Him and with you forever.

These words can be ours:

> *I love to see the temple.*
> *I'm going there someday*
> *To feel the Holy Spirit,*
> *To listen and to pray.*
> *For the temple is a house of God,*
> *A place of love and beauty.*
> *I'll prepare myself while I am young;*
> *This is my sacred duty.*[4]

I bear solemn testimony that we are children of a loving Heavenly Father. He chose His Beloved Son, Jesus Christ, to be our Savior and Redeemer. The only way to return to live with Them and with our family is through the ordinances of the holy temple. I testify that President Russell M. Nelson holds and exercises all the keys of the priesthood that make eternal life possible for all of God's children. I so testify in the sacred name of Jesus Christ, amen.

Notes

1. Doctrine and Covenants 97:15–17.
2. *Teachings of Russell M. Nelson* (2018), 369.
3. See Doctrine and Covenants 110:13–16.
4. "I Love to See the Temple," *Children's Songbook*, 95.

SATURDAY AFTERNOON SESSION

APRIL 3, 2021

NOT AS THE WORLD GIVETH

ELDER JEFFREY R. HOLLAND
Of the Quorum of the Twelve Apostles

Prior to that first Easter, as Jesus concluded the new sacramental ordinance He had administered to the Twelve, He began His majestic farewell discourse and moved toward Gethsemane, betrayal, and crucifixion. However, sensing the concern and perhaps even outright fear some of those men must have exhibited, He said this to them (*and to us*):

"Let not your heart be troubled: ye believe in God, believe also in me. . . .

"I will not leave you comfortless: I will come to you. . . .

"Peace I leave with you, my peace I give unto you: not as the world giveth, give I unto you. Let not your heart be troubled, neither let it be afraid."[1]

Challenging times come in this mortal world, including to the faithful, but the reassuring message of Christ is that although He, the paschal lamb, would go like "a sheep before [its] shearers,"[2] He would nevertheless rise, as the psalmist said, to be "our refuge and strength, [our] very present help in [times of] trouble."[3]

Realizing what difficult hours lay ahead for Christ as He moved toward the cross and for His disciples as they would take His gospel to the world in the meridian of time, go with me now to a related message for members of the Savior's Church in the latter days. It lies in the staggering number of verses in the Book of Mormon devoted to conflict of one kind or another, from Laman and Lemuel's eternally annoying behavior up to final battles involving hundreds of thousands of soldiers. One of the obvious reasons for this emphasis is that inasmuch as the Book of Mormon was written for a latter-day audience, these authors (who experienced so much of war themselves) prophetically warn us that violence and conflict will be a signature characteristic of relationships in the last days.

Of course, my theory about latter-day contention isn't very original. Two thousand years ago, the Savior warned that in the last days there would be "wars, and rumors of wars,"[4] later saying that "peace [would] be taken from the earth."[5] Surely this Prince of Peace, who taught emphatically that contention is of the devil,[6] must weep, along with His Divine Father, over those in the human family in our day who are "without affection," the scripture says, and who cannot figure out how to live together in love.[7]

Brothers and sisters, we do see too much conflict, anger, and general incivility around us. Fortunately, the current generation has not had a Third World War to fight, nor have we experienced a global economic crash like the one in 1929 leading to a Great Depression. We are, however, facing a kind of Third World War that is *not* a fight to crush our enemies but a conscription marshaling the children of God to care more about each other and to help heal the wounds we find in a conflicted world. The Great Depression we now face has less to do with the external loss of our savings and more to do with the internal loss of our self-confidence, with real deficits of faith and hope and charity all around us. But the instruments we need to create a brighter day and grow an economy of genuine goodness in society are abundantly provided for in the gospel of Jesus Christ. We cannot afford—and this *world* cannot afford—our failure to put these gospel concepts and fortifying covenants to full use personally and publicly.

So, in a world "tossed with tempest, and not comforted," as Jehovah said it would be, how do we find what He called "the covenant of . . . peace"? We find it by turning to Him who said He would have mercy on us and "with everlasting kindness" would grant peace to our children.[8] In spite of frightful prophecies and unsettling scriptures declaring that peace will be taken from the earth generally, the prophets, including our own beloved Russell M. Nelson, have taught that it does not have to be taken from us individually![9] So, this Easter let's try to practice peace in a personal way, applying the grace and healing balm of the Atonement of the Lord Jesus Christ to ourselves and our families and all those we can reach around us. Fortunately, even astonishingly, this soothing salve is made available to us "without money and without price."[10]

Such help and hope are dearly needed because in this world-wide congregation today are many who struggle with any number of challenges—physical or emotional, social or financial, or a dozen other kinds of trouble. But many of these we are *not* strong enough to address in and of ourselves, for the help and peace we need is not the kind "the world giveth."[11] No, for the truly difficult problems we need what the scriptures call "the powers of heaven," and to access these powers we must live by what these same scriptures call "principles of righteousness."[12] Now, understanding that connection between principle and power is the *one* lesson the human family never seems able to learn, so says the God of heaven and earth![13]

And what are those principles? Well, they are listed repeatedly in scripture, they are taught again and again in conferences like this, and in our dispensation, the Prophet Joseph Smith was taught them in response to *his* own version of the cry "My God, my God, why hast thou forsaken me?"[14] In the cold, uncaring confinement of Liberty Jail, he was taught that the principles of righteousness included such virtues as patience, long-suffering, gentleness, and love unfeigned.[15] Absent those principles, it was certain we would eventually face discord and enmity.

In that regard, may I speak for a moment about the *absence* in some quarters of these principles of righteousness in our time. As a rule, I am an upbeat, cheerful kind of fellow, and there is so much that is good and beautiful in our world. Certainly we have more material blessings than any generation in history, but in 21st-century culture generally and too often in the Church, we still see lives that are in trouble, with compromises resulting in too many broken covenants and too many broken hearts. Consider the coarse language that parallels sexual transgression, both of which are so omnipresent in movies or on television, or note the sexual harassment and other forms of impropriety in the workplace about which we read so much these days. In matters of covenantal purity, the sacred is too often being made common and the holy is too often being made profane. To any who are tempted to walk or talk or behave in these ways—"as the world giveth," so to speak—don't expect it to lead to peaceful experience; I promise you in the name of the Lord that it won't. "Wickedness never was happiness,"[16] an ancient prophet once said. When the dance is over, the piper must always be paid, and most often it is in a currency of tears and regret.[17]

Or perhaps we see other forms of abuse or indignity. How doubly careful we have to be as disciples of the Lord Jesus Christ not to participate in any such behavior. In no case are we to be guilty of any form of abuse or unrighteous dominion or immoral coercion—not physical or emotional or ecclesiastical or any other kind. I remember feeling the fervor of President Gordon B. Hinckley a few years ago when he spoke to the men of the Church regarding those he called "tyrants in their own homes":[18]

"How tragic and utterly disgusting a phenomenon is wife abuse," he said. "Any man in this Church who abuses his wife, who demeans her, who insults her, who exercises unrighteous dominion over her is unworthy to hold the priesthood. . . . [He] is unworthy to hold a temple recommend."[19] Equally despicable, he said, was any form of child abuse—or any other kind of abuse.[20]

In too many instances, otherwise faithful men, women, and even children can be guilty of speaking unkindly, even destructively, to those to whom they may well be sealed by a holy ordinance in the temple of the Lord. *Everyone has the right to be loved, to feel peaceful, and to find safety at home.* Please, may we try to maintain that environment there. The promise of being a peacemaker is that you will have the Holy Ghost for your constant companion and blessings will flow to you "without compulsory means" forever.[21] No one can employ a sharp tongue or unkind words and still "sing the song of redeeming love."[22]

May I close where I began. Tomorrow is Easter, a time for the righteous principles of the gospel of Jesus Christ and His Atonement to "pass over"—pass over conflict and contention, pass over despair and transgression, and ultimately pass over death. It is a time to pledge total loyalty in word and deed to the Lamb of God, who "[bore] our griefs, and carried our sorrows"[23] in His determination to finish the work of salvation in our behalf.

In spite of betrayal and pain, mistreatment and cruelty, and bearing all the accumulated sins and sorrows of the human family, the Son of the living God looked down the long path of mortality, saw us this weekend, and said: "Peace I leave with you, my peace I give unto you: not as the world giveth, give I unto you. Let not your heart be troubled, neither let it be afraid."[24] Have a blessed, joyful, peaceful Easter. Its untold possibilities have already been paid for by the Prince of Peace, whom I love with all my heart, whose Church this is, and of whom I bear unequivocal witness, even the Lord Jesus Christ, amen.

Notes

1. John 14:1, 18, 27.
2. Isaiah 53:7.
3. Psalm 46:1.
4. Joseph Smith—Matthew 1:23; see also verse 30.
5. Doctrine and Covenants 1:35.
6. See 3 Nephi 11:29.
7. Moses 7:33.
8. See Isaiah 54:8, 10–11, 13; see also 3 Nephi 22:8, 10–11, 13.
9. See Russell M. Nelson, "Blessed Are the Peacemakers," *Ensign* or *Liahona*, Nov. 2002, 39–41.
10. 2 Nephi 26:25.
11. John 14:27.
12. Doctrine and Covenants 121:36.
13. See Doctrine and Covenants 121:35.
14. See Doctrine and Covenants 121:1–6; see also Matthew 27:46.
15. See Doctrine and Covenants 121:41–42.
16. Alma 41:10.
17. See Robert Browning, "The Pied Piper of Hamelin," poetryfoundation.org.
18. See *Teachings of Presidents of the Church: Gordon B. Hinckley* (2016), 219.
19. Gordon B. Hinckley, "Personal Worthiness to Exercise the Priesthood," *Ensign*, May 2002, 54; *Liahona*, July 2002, 60.
20. See Hinckley, "Personal Worthiness to Exercise the Priesthood," *Ensign*, May 2002, 54; *Liahona*, July 2002, 60.
21. Doctrine and Covenants 121:46.
22. Alma 5:26.
23. Isaiah 53:4; see also verse 7.
24. John 14:27.

POOR LITTLE ONES

ELDER JORGE T. BECERRA
Of the Seventy

As a boy, I remember driving in the car with my father and seeing individuals on the roadside who had found themselves in difficult circumstances or who needed help. My father would always make the comment "*Pobrecito*," which means "poor little one."

On occasion, I watched with interest as my father would help many of these people, especially when we would travel to Mexico to see my grandparents. He would typically find someone in need and then go privately and provide the help they needed. I later discovered that he was helping them enroll in school, buy some food, or provide in some way or another for their well-being. He was ministering to a "poor little one" who came across his path. In fact, in my growing-up years I cannot remember a time when we did not have someone living with us who needed a place to stay as they became self-reliant. Watching these experiences created in me a spirit of compassion toward my fellow men and women and for those in need.

In *Preach My Gospel* it states: "You are surrounded by people. You pass them on the street, visit them in their homes, and travel among them. They are all children of God, your brothers and sisters. . . . Many of these people are searching for purpose in life. They are concerned for their future and their families" (*Preach My Gospel: A Guide to Missionary Service* [2018], 1).

Throughout the years, while serving in the Church, I have tried to seek after those who needed help in their lives, both temporally and spiritually. I would often hear the voice of my father saying, "*Pobrecito*," poor little one.

In the Bible we find a wonderful example of caring for a poor little one:

"Now Peter and John went up together into the temple at the hour of prayer, being the ninth hour.

"And a certain man lame from his mother's womb was carried,

whom they laid daily at the gate of the temple which is called Beautiful, to ask alms of them that entered into the temple;

"Who seeing Peter and John about to go into the temple asked an alms.

"And Peter, *fastening his eyes upon him* with John, said, Look on us.

"And he gave heed unto them, expecting to receive something of them.

"Then Peter said, Silver and gold have I none; but such as I have give I thee: In the name of Jesus Christ of Nazareth rise up and walk.

"And he took him by the right hand, and lifted him up: and immediately his feet and ankle bones received strength" (Acts 3:1–7; emphasis added).

In reading this account, I was intrigued by the use of the word *fastening*. The word *fastening* means to direct one's eyes or thoughts to or to look intently at (see "fasten," Dictionary.com). As Peter looked at this man, he saw him differently than others. He looked past his inability to walk and his weaknesses and could discern that his faith was adequate to become healed and enter into the temple to receive the blessings he was seeking.

I noticed that he took him by the right hand and lifted him up. As he assisted the man in this way, the Lord miraculously healed him, and "his feet and ankle bones received strength" (Acts 3:7). His love for this man and a desire to help him caused an increase of capacity and ability in the man who was weak.

While serving as an Area Seventy, I reserved each Tuesday night to do ministering visits with the stake presidents in my area of responsibility. I invited them to make appointments with those who were in need of an ordinance of the gospel of Jesus Christ or who were not currently keeping the covenants they had made. Through our consistent and intentional ministering, the Lord magnified our efforts and we were able to find individuals and families who were in need. These were the "poor little ones" who lived in the different stakes where we served.

On one occasion, I accompanied President Bill Whitworth, the president of the Sandy Utah Canyon View Stake, to do ministering visits. He was prayerful about whom we should visit, trying to have the same experience as Nephi, who "was led by the Spirit, not knowing beforehand the things which [he] should do" (1 Nephi 4:6). He demonstrated that as we minister, we should be led by revelation to those who are most in need, as opposed to just going down a list or visiting individuals in a methodical way. We should be led by the power of inspiration.

I remember going into the home of a young couple, Jeff and Heather, and their little boy, Kai. Jeff grew up an active member of the Church. He was a very talented athlete and had a promising career. He began to drift away from the Church in his teenage years. Later, he got into a car accident, which altered the course of his life. As we entered their home and became acquainted, Jeff asked us why we came to see his family. We responded that there were about 3,000 members who lived within the stake boundaries. I then asked him, "Jeff, of all the homes we could have visited tonight, tell us why the Lord has sent us here."

With that, Jeff became emotional and began to share with us some of his worries and some issues that they were dealing with as a family. We began to share various principles of the gospel of Jesus Christ. We invited them to do a few specific things that might seem to be challenging at first but in time would bring great happiness and joy. Then President Whitworth gave Jeff a priesthood blessing to help him overcome his challenges. Jeff and Heather agreed to do what we invited them to do.

About a year later, it was my privilege to watch Jeff baptize his wife, Heather, a member of The Church of Jesus Christ of Latter-day Saints. They are now preparing themselves to enter the temple to be sealed as a family for time and all eternity. Our visit altered the course of their lives both temporally and spiritually.

The Lord has stated:

"Wherefore, be faithful; stand in the office which I have appointed unto you; succor the weak, lift up the hands which hang down, and strengthen the feeble knees" (Doctrine and Covenants 81:5).

"And in doing these things thou wilt do the greatest good unto thy fellow beings, and wilt promote the glory of him who is your Lord" (Doctrine and Covenants 81:4).

Brothers and sisters, the Apostle Paul taught a key element in our ministering. He taught that we are all "the body of Christ, and members in particular" (1 Corinthians 12:27) and that each member of the body is needed in order to ensure that the entire body is edified. Then he taught a powerful truth that entered deeply into my heart when I read it. He said, "Much more those members of the body, which seem to be more feeble, *are necessary*: and those members of the body, which we think to be *less honourable*, upon these we bestow *more abundant honour*" (1 Corinthians 12:22–23; emphasis added).

Hence, in each ward and branch we need everyone—those who may be strong and those who are perhaps struggling. All are necessary to the vital edification of the entire "body of Christ." I often wonder who we are missing in our various congregations that would strengthen us and make us whole.

Elder D. Todd Christofferson taught: "In the Church we not only learn divine doctrine; we also experience its application. As the body of Christ, the members of the Church minister to one another in the reality of day-to-day life. All of us are imperfect. . . . In the body of Christ, we have to go beyond concepts and exalted words and have a real 'hands-on' experience as we learn to 'live together in love' [Doctrine and Covenants 42:45]" ("Why the Church," *Ensign* or *Liahona*, Nov. 2015, 108–9).

In 1849, Brigham Young had a dream in which he saw the Prophet Joseph Smith driving a large herd of sheep and goats. Some of these animals were large and beautiful; others were small and dirty. Brigham Young recalled looking into the Prophet Joseph Smith's eyes and saying, "Joseph, you have got the darndest flock . . . I ever saw in my life; what are you going to do with them?" The

Prophet, who seemed unconcerned with this unruly flock, simply replied, "[Brigham,] they are all good in their places."

When President Young awoke, he understood that while the Church would gather a variety of "sheep and goats," it was his responsibility to bring all in and allow each of them to realize their full potential as they took their places in the Church. (Adapted from Ronald W. Walker, "Brigham Young: Student of the Prophet," *Ensign*, Feb. 1998, 56–57.)

Brothers and sisters, the genesis of my talk came about as I thought deeply about *one* who is not currently engaged in the Church of Jesus Christ. For a moment I would like to speak to each one of them. Elder Neal A. Maxwell has taught that "such individuals often stay proximate to—but do not participate fully in—the Church. They will not come inside the chapel, but neither do they leave its porch. These are they who need and are needed by the Church, but who, in part, 'live without God in the world' [Mosiah 27:31]" ("Why Not Now?," *Ensign*, Nov. 1974, 12).

I would echo the invitation of our beloved President Russell M. Nelson as he first spoke to the membership of the Church. He said: "Now, to each member of the Church I say, keep on the covenant path. Your commitment to follow the Savior by making covenants with Him and then keeping those covenants will open the door to every spiritual blessing and privilege available to men, women, and children everywhere."

He then pleaded: "Now, if you have stepped off the path, may I invite you with all the hope in my heart to please come back. Whatever your concerns, whatever your challenges, there is a place for you in this, the Lord's Church. You and generations yet unborn will be blessed by your actions *now* to return to the covenant path" ("As We Go Forward Together," *Ensign* or *Liahona*, Apr. 2018, 7; emphasis added).

I bear witness of Him, even Jesus Christ, the Master Minister and Savior of us all. I invite each of us to seek out the "*pobrecitos*," the "poor little ones" among us who are in need. This is my hope and prayer in the name of Jesus Christ, amen.

INFURIATING UNFAIRNESS

ELDER DALE G. RENLUND
Of the Quorum of the Twelve Apostles

In 1994, a genocide took place in the East African country of Rwanda that was partly due to deep-seated tribal tensions. Estimates are that more than half a million people were killed.[1] Remarkably, the Rwandan people have in large part reconciled,[2] but these events continue to reverberate.

A decade ago, while visiting Rwanda, my wife and I struck up a conversation with another passenger at the Kigali airport. He lamented the unfairness of the genocide and poignantly asked, "If there were a God, wouldn't He have done something about it?" For this man—and for many of us—suffering and brutal unfairness can seem incompatible with the reality of a kind, loving Heavenly Father. Yet He is real, He is kind, and He loves each of His children perfectly. This dichotomy is as old as mankind and cannot be explained in a simple sound bite or on a bumper sticker.

To begin to make some sense of it, let us explore various types of unfairness. Consider a family in which each child received a weekly monetary allowance for doing common household chores. One son, John, purchased candy; one daughter, Anna, saved her money. Eventually, Anna bought herself a bicycle. John thought it was totally unfair that Anna got a bike when he did not. But John's choices created the inequality, not parental actions. Anna's decision to forgo the immediate gratification of eating candy did not impose any unfairness on John, because he had the same opportunity as his sister.

Our decisions can likewise yield long-term advantages or disadvantages. As the Lord revealed, "If a person gains more knowledge and intelligence in this life *through his diligence and obedience* than another, he will have so much the advantage in the world to come."[3] When others receive benefits because of their diligent choices, we cannot rightly conclude that we have been treated unfairly when we have had the same opportunity.

Another example of unfairness stems from a situation my wife,

Ruth, encountered as a child. One day Ruth learned that her mother was taking a younger sister, Merla, to buy new shoes. Ruth complained, "Mom, it's so unfair! Merla got the last new pair of shoes."

Ruth's mother asked, "Ruth, do your shoes fit?"

Ruth replied, "Well, yes."

Ruth's mother then said, "Merla's shoes no longer fit."

Ruth agreed that every child in the family should have shoes that fit. Although Ruth would have liked new shoes, her perception of being treated unfairly dissipated when she saw the circumstances through her mother's eyes.

Some unfairness cannot be explained; inexplicable unfairness is infuriating. Unfairness comes from living with bodies that are imperfect, injured, or diseased. Mortal life is inherently unfair. Some people are born in affluence; others are not. Some have loving parents; others do not. Some live many years; others, few. And on and on and on. Some individuals make injurious mistakes even when they are trying to do good. Some choose not to alleviate unfairness when they could. Distressingly, some individuals use their God-given agency to hurt others when they never should.

Different types of unfairness can merge, creating a tsunami of overwhelming unfairness. For instance, the COVID-19 pandemic disproportionately affects those who already are subject to multifactorial, underlying disadvantages. My heart aches for those who face such unfairness, but I declare with all my aching heart that Jesus Christ both understands unfairness and has the power to provide a remedy. Nothing compares to the unfairness He endured. It was not fair that He experienced all the pains and afflictions of mankind. It was not fair that He suffered for my sins and mistakes and for yours. But He chose to do so because of His love for us and for Heavenly Father. He understands perfectly what we are experiencing.[4]

Scripture records that ancient Israelites complained that God was treating them unfairly. In response, Jehovah asked, "For can a woman forget her sucking child, that she should not have compassion on the son of her womb?" As unlikely as it is that a loving mother would forget her infant child, Jehovah declared that His devotion was even more steadfast. He affirmed: "Yea, they may forget, yet will I not forget thee. . . . Behold, I have graven thee upon the palms of my hands; thy walls are continually before me."[5] Because Jesus Christ endured the infinite atoning sacrifice, He empathizes perfectly with us.[6] He is always aware of us and our circumstances.

In mortality, we can "come boldly" to the Savior and receive compassion, healing, and help.[7] Even while we suffer inexplicably, God can bless us in simple, ordinary, and significant ways. As we learn to recognize these blessings, our trust in God will increase. In the eternities, Heavenly Father and Jesus Christ will resolve all unfairness. We understandably want to know *how* and *when*. *How* are They going to do that? *When* are They going to do it? To my knowledge, They have not revealed *how* or *when*.[8] What I do know is that They *will*.

In unfair situations, one of our tasks is to trust that "all that is unfair about life can be made right through the Atonement of Jesus Christ."[9] Jesus Christ overcame the world and "absorbed" all unfairness. Because of Him, we can have peace in this world and be of good cheer.[10] If we let Him, Jesus Christ will consecrate the unfairness for our gain.[11] He will not just console us and restore what was lost;[12] He will use the unfairness for our benefit. When it comes to *how* and *when*, we need to recognize and accept, as did Alma, that "it mattereth not; for God knoweth all these things; and it sufficeth me to know that this is the case."[13]

We can try to hold our questions about *how* and *when* for later and focus on developing faith in Jesus Christ, that He has both the power to make everything right and yearns to do so.[14] For us to insist on knowing *how* or *when* is unproductive and, after all, myopic.[15]

As we develop faith in Jesus Christ, we should also strive to become like Him. We then approach others with compassion and try to alleviate unfairness where we find it;[16] we can try to make things right within our sphere of influence. Indeed, the Savior directed that we "should be anxiously engaged in a good cause, and do many things of [our] own free will, and bring to pass much righteousness."[17]

Someone who has been anxiously engaged in combating unfairness is attorney Bryan Stevenson. His legal practice in the United States is dedicated to defending the wrongly accused, ending excessive punishment, and protecting basic human rights. Some years ago, Mr. Stevenson defended a man who had been falsely accused of murder and was condemned to die. Mr. Stevenson asked the man's local Christian church for support, even though the man was not active in his church and was disparaged in the community due to a widely known extramarital affair.

To focus the congregation on what really mattered, Mr. Stevenson spoke to them about the woman accused of adultery who was brought to Jesus. The accusers wanted to stone her to death, but Jesus said, "He that is without sin . . . , let him first cast a stone at her."[18] The woman's accusers withdrew. Jesus did not condemn the woman but charged her to sin no more.[19]

After recounting this episode, Mr. Stevenson observed that self-righteousness, fear, and anger have caused even Christians to hurl stones at people who stumble. He then said, "We can't simply watch that happen," and he encouraged the congregants to become "stonecatchers."[20] Brothers and sisters, not throwing stones is the first step in treating others with compassion. The second step is to try to catch stones thrown by others.

How we deal with advantages and disadvantages is part of life's test. We will be judged not so much by what we say but by how we treat the vulnerable and disadvantaged.[21] As Latter-day Saints, we seek to follow the Savior's example, to go about doing good.[22] We demonstrate our love for our neighbor by working to ensure the dignity of all Heavenly Father's children.

With our own advantages and disadvantages in mind, reflection is healthy. For John to understand why Anna got the bike was revealing. For Ruth to view Merla's need for shoes through her mother's eyes was enlightening. To try to see things with an eternal perspective can be clarifying. As we become more like the Savior, we develop more empathy, understanding, and charity.

I return to the question posed by our fellow passenger in Kigali when he lamented the unfairness of the Rwandan genocide and asked, "If there were a God, wouldn't He have done something about it?"

Without minimizing the suffering caused by the genocide, and after acknowledging our inability to comprehend such suffering, we replied that Jesus Christ has done something about infuriating unfairness.[23] We explained many gospel precepts concerning Jesus Christ and the Restoration of His Church.[24]

Afterward, our acquaintance asked, with tears in his eyes, "You mean there is something I can do for my dead parents and uncle?"

We said, "Oh, yes!" We then testified that all that is unfair about life can be made right through the Atonement of Jesus Christ and that by His authority families can be joined together forever.

When faced with unfairness, we can push ourselves away from God or we can be drawn toward Him for help and support. For example, the prolonged warfare between the Nephites and the Lamanites affected people differently. Mormon observed that "many had become hardened" while others "were softened because of their afflictions, insomuch that they did humble themselves before God."[25]

Do not let unfairness harden you or corrode your faith in God. Instead, ask God for help. Increase your appreciation for and reliance on the Savior. Rather than becoming bitter, let Him help you become better.[26] Allow Him to help you persevere, to let your afflictions be "swallowed up in the joy of Christ."[27] Join Him in His mission "to heal the brokenhearted,"[28] strive to mitigate unfairness, and become a stonecatcher.[29]

I testify that the Savior lives. He understands unfairness. The marks in the palms of His hands continually remind Him of you and your circumstances. He ministers to you in all your distress. For those who come unto Him, a crown of beauty will replace the ashes of mourning; joy and gladness will replace grief and sorrow;

appreciation and celebration will replace discouragement and despair.[30] Your faith in Heavenly Father and Jesus Christ will be rewarded more than you can imagine. All unfairness—especially infuriating unfairness—will be consecrated for your gain. I so testify in the name of Jesus Christ, amen.

Notes

1. See John Reader, *Africa: A Biography of the Continent* (1999), 635–36, 673–79.
2. Though hopeful, the Rwandan reconciliation is complex. Some question its depth and durability. See, for example, "The Great Rwanda Debate: Paragon or Prison?," *Economist*, Mar. 27, 2021, 41–43.
3. Doctrine and Covenants 130:19; emphasis added.
4. See Hebrews 4:15.
5. 1 Nephi 21:15–16.
6. See Alma 7:11–13.
7. See Hebrews 4:16; see also Isaiah 41:10; 43:2; 46:4; 61:1–3.
8. A word of caution: We should resist the temptation to create our own theories as to *how* and *when*, regardless of how well reasoned or plausible. We cannot justifiably fill the void for what God has not yet revealed.
9. *Preach My Gospel: A Guide to Missionary Service* (2018), 52; see also Isaiah 61:2–3; Revelation 21:4. "All that is unfair about life can be made right" likely means that the consequences of unfairness to us will be resolved, mitigated, or lifted. In his final general conference talk, "Come What May, and Love It," Elder Joseph B. Wirthlin said: "Every tear today will eventually be returned a hundredfold with tears of rejoicing and gratitude. . . . A principle of compensation prevails" (*Ensign* or *Liahona*, Nov. 2008, 28).
10. See John 16:33.
11. See 2 Nephi 2:2.
12. See Job 42:10, 12–13; Jacob 3:1.
13. Alma 40:5.
14. See Mosiah 4:9.
15. See Russell M. Nelson, "Let God Prevail," *Ensign* or *Liahona*, Nov. 2020, 93. *Myopic* means nearsighted.
16. For example, Captain Moroni affirmed that it is wrong for individuals to stand by and "do nothing" when they can assist others (see Alma 60:9–11; see also 2 Corinthians 1:3–4).
17. Doctrine and Covenants 58:27; see also verses 26, 28–29.
18. John 8:7.
19. See John 8:10–11; the Joseph Smith Translation of verse 11 includes, "And the woman glorified God from that hour, and believed on his name," suggesting that the Savior's lack of condemnation and His commandment to "sin no more" impacted the rest of the woman's life.
20. Bryan Stevenson, *Just Mercy: A Story of Justice and Redemption* (2015), 308–9.
21. See Matthew 25:31–46.
22. See Acts 10:38; see also Russell M. Nelson, "The Second Great Commandment," *Ensign* or *Liahona*, Nov. 2019, 96–100.
23. See Doctrine and Covenants 1:17, 22–23.
24. These precepts are clearly articulated in "The Restoration of the Fulness of the Gospel of Jesus Christ: A Bicentennial Proclamation to the World," ChurchofJesusChrist.org.
25. Alma 62:41.
26. See Amos C. Brown, in Boyd Matheson, "'It Can Be Well with This Nation' If We Lock Arms as Children of God," *Church News*, July 25, 2019, thechurchnews.com.
27. Alma 31:38.
28. See Luke 4:16–19. To heal the brokenhearted is to restore those whose mind, will, intellect, or inner self has been shattered or crushed (see James Strong, *The New Strong's Expanded Exhaustive Concordance of the Bible* [2010], Hebrew dictionary section, 139 and 271).

29. See, for instance, Russell M. Nelson, "Let God Prevail," *Ensign* or *Liahona*, Nov. 2020, 94; Dallin H. Oaks, "Love Your Enemies," *Ensign* or *Liahona*, Nov. 2020, 26–29. President Nelson exhorted: "Today I call upon our members everywhere to lead out in abandoning attitudes and actions of prejudice. I plead with you to promote respect for all of God's children." This is more than just being opposed to attitudes and actions of prejudice. President Oaks quoted the Reverend Theresa A. Dear: "Racism thrives on hatred, oppression, collusion, passivity, indifference and silence." Then he said, "As members of The Church of Jesus Christ of Latter-day Saints, we must do better to help root out racism."

30. See Isaiah 61:3. Receiving a crown of beauty means that we become joint-heirs with Jesus Christ in the kingdom of God. See also Donald W. Parry, Jay A. Parry, and Tina M. Peterson, *Understanding Isaiah* (1998), 541–43.

THE PERSONAL JOURNEY
OF A CHILD OF GOD

ELDER NEIL L. ANDERSEN

Of the Quorum of the Twelve Apostles

Each of us has been affected by the worldwide pandemic, as family and friends have unexpectedly moved beyond mortality. Let me acknowledge three we dearly miss, representing all those we love so much.

Brother Philippe Nsondi was serving as the patriarch of the Brazzaville Republic of Congo Stake when he passed away. He was a medical doctor who shared his talents generously with others.[1]

Sister Clara Elisa Ruano de Villareal from Tulcán, Ecuador, embraced the restored gospel at age 34 and was a beloved leader. Her family said goodbye singing her favorite hymn, "I Know That My Redeemer Lives."[2]

And Brother Ray Tuineau from Utah. His wife, Juliet, said, "I want [my boys] to [remember that their dad] always tried to put God first."[3]

The Lord has said, "Thou shalt live together in love, insomuch that thou shalt weep for the loss of them that die."[4]

While we weep, we also rejoice in the glorious Resurrection of our Savior. Because of Him, our loved ones and friends continue their eternal journey. As President Joseph F. Smith explained: "We can not forget them; we do not cease to love them. . . . They have advanced; we are advancing; we are growing as they have grown."[5] President Russell M. Nelson said, "Our tears of sorrow . . . turn to tears of anticipation."[6]

We Know about Life before Birth

Our eternal perspective not only enlarges our understanding of those who are continuing their journey beyond mortality but also opens our understanding of those who are earlier in their journey and just now entering mortality.

Each person who comes to earth is a unique son or daughter of

God.[7] Our personal journey did not begin at birth. Before we were born, we were together in a world of preparation where we "received [our] first lessons in the world of spirits."[8] Jehovah told Jeremiah, "Before I formed thee in the belly I knew thee; and before thou camest forth out of the womb I sanctified thee."[9]

Some may question if life begins with the formation of an embryo, or when the heart begins to beat, or when the baby can live outside of the womb, but for us, there is no question that spirit daughters and sons of God are on their own personal journeys coming to earth to receive a body and experience mortality.

As covenant children of God, we love, honor, nurture, safeguard, and welcome those spirits who are coming from the premortal world.

The Amazing Contribution of Women

For a woman, having a child can be a great sacrifice physically, emotionally, and economically. We love and honor the amazing women of this Church. With intelligence and wisdom, you bear the burdens of your family. You love. You serve. You sacrifice. You strengthen faith, minister to those in need, and greatly contribute to society.

The Sacred Responsibility of Safeguarding Life

Years ago, feeling deep concern for the number of abortions in the world, President Gordon B. Hinckley addressed the women of the Church with words that are relevant for us today. He said: "You who are wives and mothers are the anchors of the family. You bear the children. What an enormous and sacred responsibility that is. . . . What is happening to our appreciation of the sanctity of human life? Abortion is an evil, stark and real and repugnant, which is sweeping over the earth. I plead with the women of this Church to shun it, to stand above it, to stay away from those compromising situations which make it appear desirable. There may be some few circumstances under which it can occur, but they are extremely limited.[10] . . . You are the mothers of the sons and daughters of God, whose lives are sacred. Safeguarding them is a divinely given responsibility which cannot be lightly brushed aside."[11]

Elder Marcus B. Nash shared with me the story of a dear 84-year-old woman who, during her baptismal interview, "acknowledged an abortion [many years before]." With heartfelt emotion, she said: "I have carried the burden of having aborted a child every day of my life for forty-six years. . . . Nothing I did would take the pain and guilt away. I was hopeless until I was taught the true gospel of Jesus Christ. I learned how to repent . . . and suddenly I was filled with hope. I finally came to know that I could be forgiven if I truly repented of my sins."[12]

How grateful we are for the divine gifts of repentance and forgiveness.

What Can We Do?

What is our responsibility as peaceful disciples of Jesus Christ? Let us live God's commandments, teach them to our children, and share them with others who are willing to listen.[13] Let us share our deep feelings about the sanctity of life with those who make decisions in society. They may not fully appreciate what we believe, but we pray that they will more fully understand why, for us, these decisions go well beyond just what a person wants for his or her own life.

If an unanticipated child is expected, let us reach out with love, encouragement, and, when needed, financial help, strengthening a mother in allowing her child to be born and continue his or her journey in mortality.[14]

The Beauty of Adoption

In our family, we have been immeasurably blessed as two decades ago, a young 16-year-old learned that she was expecting a child. She and the baby's father were not married, and they could see no way forward together. The young woman believed the life she was carrying was precious. She gave birth to a baby girl and allowed a righteous family to adopt her as their own. For Bryce and

Jolinne, she was an answer to their prayers. They named her Emily and taught her to trust in her Heavenly Father and in His Son, Jesus Christ.

Emily grew up. How grateful we are that Emily and our grandson, Christian, fell in love and were married in the house of the Lord. Emily and Christian now have their own little girl.

Emily recently wrote: "Throughout these last nine months of pregnancy, I had time to reflect on the events [of] my own birth. I thought of my birth mother, who was just 16 years old. As I experienced the aches and changes that pregnancy brings, I couldn't help but imagine how difficult it would have been at the young age of 16. . . . The tears flow even now as I think of my birth mother, who knew she couldn't give me the life [she desired for me and unselfishly placed] me for adoption. I can't fathom what she might have gone through in those nine months—being watched with judging eyes as her body changed, the teen experiences she missed, knowing that at the end of this labor of motherly love, she would place her child into the arms of another. I am so thankful for her selfless choice, that she did not choose to use her agency in a way that would take away my own." Emily concludes, "I'm so thankful for Heavenly Father's divine plan, for my incredible parents who [loved and cared for] me, and for temples where we can be sealed to our families for eternity."[15]

The Savior "took a child, and set him in the midst of them: and when he had taken him in his arms, he said unto them, Whosoever shall receive one of [these] children in my name, receiveth me."[16]

When Righteous Desires Are Not Yet Realized

I express my love and compassion for righteous couples who marry and are unable to have the children they so eagerly anticipate and to those women and men who have not had the opportunity to marry according to God's law. The unrealized dreams of life are difficult to understand if viewed only from the perspective of mortality. As the Lord's servant, I promise you that as you are faithful to Jesus Christ and your covenants, you will receive compensating blessings in this life and your righteous desires in the eternal time line of the Lord.[17] There can be happiness in the journey of mortality even when all of our righteous hopes are not realized.[18]

After birth, children continue to need our help. Some need it desperately. Each year through caring bishops and your generous contributions of fast offerings and humanitarian funds, the lives of millions and millions of children are blessed. The First Presidency recently announced an additional 20 million dollars to assist UNICEF in their global efforts to administer two billion vaccines.[19] Children are loved by God.

The Sacred Decision to Have a Child

It is concerning that even in some of the most prosperous countries of the world, fewer children are being born.[20] "God's commandment for His children to multiply and replenish the earth remains in force."[21] When to have a child and how many children to have are private decisions to be made between a husband and wife and the Lord. With faith and prayer, these sacred decisions can be beautiful, revelatory experiences.[22]

I share the story of the Laing family of Southern California. Sister Rebecca Laing writes:

"In the summer of 2011, life for our family was seemingly perfect. We were happily married with four children—ages 9, 7, 5, and 3. . . .

"My pregnancies and deliveries [had been] high risk . . . [and] we felt [very] blessed to have four children, [thinking] that our family was complete. In October while listening to general conference, I felt an unmistakable feeling that we were to have another baby. As LeGrand and I pondered and prayed, . . . we knew that God had a different plan for us than we had for ourselves.

"After another difficult pregnancy and delivery, we were blessed with a beautiful baby girl. We named her Brielle. She was a miracle. Moments after her birth, while still in [the delivery room], I heard the unmistakable voice of the Spirit: 'There is one more.'

"Three years later, another miracle, Mia. Brielle and Mia are a tremendous joy for our family." She concludes, "Being open to the Lord's direction and following His plan for us will always bring greater happiness than . . . relying on our own understanding."[23]

The Savior loves each precious child.

"And he took their little children, one by one, and blessed them. . . .

"And . . . they cast their eyes towards heaven, . . . and they saw angels descending out of heaven . . . in the midst of fire; and [the angels] . . . encircled those little ones about, . . . and the angels did minister unto them."[24]

I testify that your own personal journey as a child of God did not begin for you as the first flow of earth's air came rushing into your lungs, and it will not end when you take your last breath of mortality.

May we always remember that each spirit child of God is coming to earth on his or her own personal journey.[25] May we welcome them, safeguard them, and always love them. As you receive these precious children in the Savior's name and help them in their eternal journey, I promise you that the Lord will bless you and shower His love and approval upon you. In the name of Jesus Christ, amen.

Notes

1. Personal correspondence.
2. Personal correspondence. See "I Know That My Redeemer Lives," *Hymns*, no. 136.
3. Personal correspondence.
4. Doctrine and Covenants 42:45.
5. Joseph F. Smith, in Conference Report, Apr. 1916, 3.
6. In Trent Toone, "'A Fulness of Joy': President Nelson Shares Message of Eternal Life at His Daughter's Funeral," *Church News*, Jan. 19, 2019, thechurchnews.com.
7. See "The Family: A Proclamation to the World," ChurchofJesusChrist.org.
8. Doctrine and Covenants 138:56.
9. Jeremiah 1:5. The New Testament tells of the unborn John the Baptist leaping in the womb as Elisabeth encountered Mary, who was expecting the baby Jesus (see Luke 1:41).
10. The official position of The Church of Jesus Christ of Latter-day Saints:
    "The Church of Jesus Christ of Latter-day Saints believes in the sanctity of human life. Therefore, the Church opposes elective abortion for personal or social convenience, and counsels its members not to submit to, perform, encourage, pay for, or arrange for such abortions.
    "The Church allows for possible exceptions for its members when:
    "Pregnancy results from rape or incest, or
    "A competent physician determines that the life or health of the mother is in serious jeopardy, or
    "A competent physician determines that the fetus has severe defects that will not allow the baby to survive beyond birth.
    "The Church teaches its members that even these rare exceptions do not justify abortion

automatically. Abortion is a most serious matter and should be considered only after the persons involved have consulted with their local church leaders and feel through personal prayer that their decision is correct.

"The Church has not favored or opposed legislative proposals or public demonstrations concerning abortion" ("Abortion," Newsroom, newsroom.ChurchofJesusChrist.org; see also *General Handbook: Serving in The Church of Jesus Christ of Latter-day Saints*, 38.6.1, ChurchofJesusChrist.org).

11. Gordon B. Hinckley, "Walking in the Light of the Lord," *Ensign*, Nov. 1998, 99; *Liahona*, Jan. 1999, 117. President Gordon B. Hinckley said:

"Abortion is an ugly thing, a debasing thing, a thing which inevitably brings remorse and sorrow and regret.

"While we denounce it, we make allowance in such circumstances as when pregnancy is the result of incest or rape, when the life or health of the mother is judged by competent medical authority to be in serious jeopardy, or when the fetus is known by competent medical authority to have serious defects that will not allow the baby to survive beyond birth.

"But such instances are rare, and there is only a negligible probability of their occurring. In these circumstances those who face the question are asked to consult with their local ecclesiastical leaders and to pray in great earnestness, receiving a confirmation through prayer before proceeding" ("What Are People Asking about Us?," *Ensign*, Nov. 1998, 71; *Liahona*, Jan. 1999, 83–84).

12. See Neil L. Andersen, *The Divine Gift of Forgiveness* (2019), 25.

On one occasion in France, during a baptismal interview, a woman spoke to me of her abortion of many years before. I was grateful for her goodness. She was baptized. About a year later, I received a phone call. This wonderful woman in the year since her baptism had been taught by the Holy Ghost. She called, sobbing: "Do you remember . . . I told you about an abortion from years before? I felt sorry for what I had done. But [this] past year has changed me. . . . My heart has been turned to the Savior. . . . I am so pained by the seriousness of my sin that I have no way to restore."

I felt the Lord's immense love for this woman. President Boyd K. Packer said: "Restoring what you cannot restore, healing the wound you cannot heal, fixing that which you broke and you cannot fix is the very purpose of the atonement of Christ. When your desire is firm and you are willing to pay the 'uttermost farthing' [see Matthew 5:25–26], the law of restitution is suspended. Your obligation is transferred to the Lord. He will settle your accounts" ("The Brilliant Morning of Forgiveness," *Ensign*, Nov. 1995, 19–20). I assured her of the Savior's love. The Lord not only lifted the sin from her; He strengthened and refined her spirit. (See Neil L. Andersen, *The Divine Gift of Forgiveness*, 154–56.)

13. See Dallin H. Oaks, "Protect the Children," *Ensign* or *Liahona*, Nov. 2012, 43–46.

14. Safeguarding the lives of a daughter or son of God is also the responsibility of the father. Every father has an emotional, spiritual, and financial responsibility to welcome, love, and care for the child coming to earth.

15. Personal correspondence.

16. Mark 9:36–37.

17. See Neil L. Andersen, "A Compensatory Spiritual Power for the Righteous" (Brigham Young University devotional, Aug. 18, 2015), speeches.byu.edu.

18. See Dallin H. Oaks, "The Great Plan of Happiness," *Ensign*, Nov. 1993, 75; see also Russell M. Nelson, "Choices," *Ensign*, Nov. 1990, 75.

19. See "Bishop Caussé Thanks UNICEF and Church Members for COVID-19 Relief," Newsroom, Mar. 5, 2021, newsroom.ChurchofJesusChrist.org.

20. For example, if the United States had maintained its fertility rate of 2008, just 13 years ago, there would be 5.8 million more children alive today (see Lyman Stone, "5.8 Million Fewer Babies: America's Lost Decade in Fertility," Institute for Family Studies, Feb. 3, 2021, ifstudies .org/blog).

21. "The Family: A Proclamation to the World," ChurchofJesusChrist.org. The scriptures record that "children are an heritage of the Lord" (Psalm 127:3). See Russell M. Nelson, "How Firm Our Foundation," *Ensign*, May 2002, 75–76; *Liahona*, July 2002, 83–84; see also Dallin H. Oaks, "Truth and the Plan," *Ensign* or *Liahona*, Nov. 2018, 27.

22. See Neil L. Andersen, "Children," *Ensign* or *Liahona*, Nov. 2011, 28.

23. Personal correspondence, Mar. 10, 2021.
24. 3 Nephi 17:21, 24.
25. "In reality, we are all travelers—even explorers of mortality. We do not have the benefit of previous personal experience. We must pass over steep precipices and turbulent waters in our own journey here on earth" (Thomas S. Monson, "The Bridge Builder," *Ensign* or *Liahona*, Nov. 2003, 67).

YE SHALL BE FREE

ELDER THIERRY K. MUTOMBO
Of the Seventy

My beloved brothers and sisters, I'm so grateful for the privilege to address you from Africa. It is a blessing to have the technology today and to use it in the most effective way to reach out to you wherever you are.

In September 2019, Sister Mutombo and I, while serving as leaders of the Maryland Baltimore Mission, had the privilege to visit some Church history sites in Palmyra, New York, while attending a mission leadership seminar. We ended our visit in the Sacred Grove. Our intention in visiting the Sacred Grove was not to have a special manifestation or a vision, but we did feel God's presence in this sacred place. Our hearts were filled with gratitude for the Prophet Joseph Smith.

On the way back, Sister Mutombo noticed that I had a big smile while driving, so she asked, "What is the reason for your excitement?"

I responded, "My dear Nathalie, the truth will always triumph over error, and darkness will not continue on earth because of the restored gospel of Jesus Christ."

God the Father and Jesus Christ visited the young Joseph Smith to bring to the light what was hidden so we may receive the "knowledge of things as they are, . . . as they were, and as they [will be]" (Doctrine and Covenants 93:24).

After over 200 years, many still seek the truths needed to become free of some of the traditions and the lies that the adversary spreads throughout the world. Many are "blinded by the subtle craftiness of men" (Doctrine and Covenants 123:12). In his Epistle to the Ephesians, Paul taught, "Awake thou that sleepest, and arise from the dead, and Christ shall give thee light" (Ephesians 5:14). The Savior promised that He will be the light unto all who hear His words (see 2 Nephi 10:14).

Thirty-five years ago, my parents were also blinded and were desperately seeking to know the truth and were concerned about where to turn to find it. My parents were both born in the village, where the traditions were rooted in individuals' and families' lives. They both left their village when they were young and came to the city, looking for a better life.

They married and started their family in a very modest way. We were almost eight people in a small house—my parents, two of my sisters and I, and a cousin who used to live with us. I was wondering if we were truly a family, as we were not permitted to have dinner at the same table with our parents. When our dad returned from work, as soon as he entered the house, we were asked to leave and to go outside. Our nights were very short, as we could not sleep because of the lack of harmony and true love in our parents' marriage. Our home was not only small in size, but it was a dark place. Before meeting with the missionaries, we attended different churches every Sunday. It was clear that our parents were seeking for something that the world could not provide.

This went on until we met with Elder and Sister Hutchings, the first senior missionary couple called to serve in Zaire (known today as DR of Congo or Congo-Kinshasa). When we started meeting with these wonderful missionaries, who were like angels that came from God, I noticed that something started to change in our family. After our baptism, we truly started to progressively have a new lifestyle because of the restored gospel. The words of Christ began to enlarge our souls. They began to enlighten our understanding and became delicious to us, as the truths that we received were discernible and we could see the light, and this light grew brighter and brighter daily.

This understanding of the *why* of the gospel was helping us to become more like the Savior. The size of our home did not change; neither did our social conditions. But I witnessed a change of heart in my parents as we prayed daily, morning and evening. We studied the Book of Mormon; we held family home evening; we truly became a family. Every Sunday we woke up at 6:00 a.m. to prepare to go to church, and we would travel for hours to attend Church meetings every week without complaining. It was a wonderful experience to witness. We, who had previously walked in darkness, chased darkness from among us (see Doctrine and Covenants 50:25) and saw "great light" (2 Nephi 19:2).

I remember one day when I was not willing to wake up early in the morning for our family prayer, I murmured to my sisters, "There is truly nothing else that we can do in this home, only pray, pray, pray." My dad heard my comments. I remember his reaction as he lovingly but firmly taught me, "As long as you will be in this house, you will pray, pray, pray."

My father's words sounded in my ears daily. What do you think Sister Mutombo and I do with our children today? We pray, pray, and pray. This is our legacy.

The man who was born blind and was healed by Jesus Christ, after being pressured by his neighbors and the Pharisees, said:

"A man that is called Jesus made clay, and anointed mine eyes, and said unto me, Go to the pool of Siloam, and wash: and I went and washed, and I received sight. . . .

". . . One thing [that] I know [is] that, whereas I was blind, now I [can] see" (John 9:11, 25).

We also were blind and can now see. The restored gospel has impacted our family since that time. Understanding the *why* of the gospel has blessed three generations of my family and will continue to bless many generations to come.

Jesus Christ is the light that shines in darkness. Those who follow Him "shall not walk in darkness, but shall have the light of life" (John 8:12).

For almost a year, between 2016 and 2017, the people in the Kasai region faced a terrible tragedy. It was a very dark period for the people because of a conflict between a traditional group of warriors and government forces. The violence spread from towns in Kasai-Central Province to the wider Kasai region. Many people fled their homes for safety and hid in the bush. They had no food or water or not anything, really, and among these were some members of The

Church of Jesus Christ of Latter-day Saints in the Kananga area. Some members of the Church were killed by the militia.

Brother Honoré Mulumba of the Nganza Ward in Kananga and his family were some of the few people who remained hidden in their house, not knowing where to go because all the streets were transformed into firing ranges. One day some neighborhood militiamen had noticed the presence of Brother Mulumba and his family as one evening they went out to try to find some vegetables in the family garden to eat. A group of the militiamen came to their home and then pulled them out and told them to choose to adhere to their militia practices or be killed.

Brother Mulumba courageously told them, "I'm a member of The Church of Jesus Christ of Latter-day Saints. My family and I have accepted Jesus Christ and have faith in Him. We will remain faithful to our covenants and will accept to die."

They told them, "As you have chosen Jesus Christ, your bodies will be eaten by the dogs," and they promised to come back. But they never did come back, and the family stayed there for two months and never saw them again. Brother Mulumba and his family kept the torch of their faith alight. They remembered their covenants and were protected.

Jesus Christ is the light that we should hold up even during the dark times of our mortal life (see 3 Nephi 18:24). When we choose to follow Christ, we choose to be changed. A man or woman changed for Christ will be captained by Christ, and we will be asking, as Paul did, "Lord, what wilt thou have me to do?" (Acts 9:6). We will "follow his steps" (1 Peter 2:21). We will "walk, even as he walked" (1 John 2:6). (See Ezra Taft Benson, "Born of God," *Ensign*, July 1989, 2, 4; *Tambuli*, Oct. 1989, 2, 6.)

I testify of Him who died, was buried, and rose again the third day and ascended into heaven so that you and I receive the blessings of immortality and exaltation. He is "the light, . . . the life, and the truth" (Ether 4:12). He is the antidote and remedy to the confusion of the world. He is the standard of excellence for exaltation, even Jesus Christ. In the name of Jesus Christ, amen.

HOPE IN CHRIST

PRESIDENT M. RUSSELL BALLARD
Acting President of the Quorum of the Twelve Apostles

Brothers and sisters, at this Easter time we focus on the glorious Resurrection of our Lord and Savior, Jesus Christ. We remember His loving invitation to "come unto me, all ye that labour and are heavy laden, and I will give you rest.

"Take my yoke upon you, and learn of me; for I am meek and lowly in heart: and ye shall find rest unto your souls.

"For my yoke is easy, and my burden is light."[1]

The Savior's invitation to come unto Him is an invitation to all not only to come unto Him but also to belong to His Church.

In the verse preceding this loving invitation, Jesus teaches how this is done by seeking to follow Him. He declared, "No man [or woman] knoweth the Son, but the Father; neither knoweth any man [or woman] the Father, save the Son, and he [or she] to whomsoever the Son will reveal him."[2]

Jesus wants us to know God is a loving Heavenly Father.

Knowing that we are loved by our Heavenly Father will help us know who we are and know that we belong to His great eternal family.

The Mayo Clinic recently noted: "Having a sense of belonging is so important. . . . Nearly every aspect of our lives is organized around belonging to something." This report adds, "We cannot separate the importance of a sense of belonging from our physical and mental health"[3]—and, I would add, our spiritual health.

On the evening before His suffering in Gethsemane and death on the cross, the Savior met with His disciples for the Last Supper. He said to them, "In the world *ye shall have tribulation*: but be of good cheer; I have overcome the world."[4] Before sunset the following day, Jesus Christ had suffered and had "died [on the cross] for our sins."[5]

I wonder how lonely the faithful women and men who followed

Him must have felt in Jerusalem as the sun set and darkness and fear encompassed them.[6]

Like these ancient disciples nearly 2,000 years ago, many of you may also feel lonely from time to time. I have experienced this loneliness since the death of my precious wife, Barbara, over two and a half years ago. I know what it is to be surrounded by family members, friends, and associates but still feel lonely—because the love of my life is no longer here beside me.

The COVID-19 pandemic has highlighted this sense of isolation and loneliness for many. Nevertheless, despite the challenges we face in life, we can, like on that first Easter morning, awake to a new life in Christ, with new and marvelous possibilities and new realities as we turn to the Lord for hope and belonging.

I personally feel the pain of those who lack a sense of belonging. As I watch news from around the world, I see many who seem to be experiencing this loneliness. I think that, for many, it is because they may not know that they are loved by Heavenly Father and that we all belong to His eternal family. Believing that God loves us and that we are His children is comforting and assuring.

Because we are the spirit children of God, everyone has a divine origin, nature, and potential. Each of us "is a beloved spirit son or daughter of heavenly parents."[7] This is our identity! This is who we really are!

Our spiritual identity is enhanced as we understand our many mortal identities, including ethnic, cultural, or national heritage.

This sense of spiritual and cultural identity, love, and belonging can inspire hope and love for Jesus Christ.

I speak of hope in Christ not as wishful thinking. Instead, I speak of hope as an expectation that will be realized. Such hope is essential to overcoming adversity, fostering spiritual resilience and strength, and coming to know that we are loved by our Eternal Father and that we are His children, who belong to His family.

When we have hope in Christ, we come to know that as we need to make and keep sacred covenants, our fondest desires and dreams can be fulfilled through Him.

The Quorum of the Twelve Apostles have counseled together in a spirit of prayer and with a yearning to understand how to help all who feel alone or feel they don't belong. We long to help all who feel this way. Let me mention, in particular, those who are currently single.

Brothers and sisters, more than half of adults in the Church today are widowed, divorced, or not yet married. Some wonder about their opportunities and place in God's plan and in the Church. We should understand that eternal life is not simply a question of current marital status but of discipleship and being "valiant in the testimony of Jesus."[8] The hope of all who are single is the same as for all members of the Lord's restored Church—access to the grace of Christ through "obedience to the laws and ordinances of the Gospel."[9]

May I suggest that there are some important principles we need to understand.

First, scriptures and latter-day prophets confirm that everyone who is faithful in keeping gospel covenants will have the opportunity for exaltation. President Russell M. Nelson taught: "In the Lord's own way and time, no blessing will be withheld from His faithful Saints. The Lord will judge and reward each individual according to heartfelt desire as well as deed."[10]

Second, the precise time and manner in which the blessings of exaltation are bestowed have not all been revealed, but they are nonetheless assured.[11] President Dallin H. Oaks explained that some of the circumstances "of mortality will be set right in the Millennium, which is the time for fulfilling all that is incomplete in the great plan of happiness for all of our Father's worthy children."[12]

That doesn't mean that every blessing is deferred until the Millennium; some have already been received, and others will continue to be received until that day.[13]

Third, waiting upon the Lord implies continued obedience and spiritual progress toward Him. Waiting upon the Lord does not imply biding one's time. You should never feel like you are in a *waiting* room.

Waiting upon the Lord implies action. I have learned over the years that our hope in Christ increases when we serve others. Serving as Jesus served, we naturally increase our hope in Him.

The personal growth one can achieve now while waiting upon the Lord and His promises is an invaluable, sacred element of His plan for each one of us. The contributions one can make now to help build up the Church on earth and to gather Israel are much needed. Marital status has nothing to do with one's capacity to serve. The Lord honors those who serve and wait upon Him in patience and faith.[14]

Fourth, God offers eternal life to all of His children. All those who accept the Savior's gracious gift of repentance and live His commandments will receive eternal life, even though they do not attain to all its characteristics and perfections in mortality. Those who repent will experience the Lord's readiness to forgive, as He has assured: "Yea, and as often as my people repent will I forgive them their trespasses against me."[15]

In the final analysis, a person's capacity, desires, and opportunities in matters of agency and choice, including qualification for eternal blessings, are matters only the Lord can judge.

Fifth, our confidence in these assurances is rooted in our faith in Jesus Christ, by whose grace all things pertaining to mortality are set right.[16] All promised blessings are made possible through Him, who, by His Atonement, "descended below all things"[17] and has "overcome the world."[18] He "hath sat down on the right hand of God, to claim of the Father his rights of mercy which he hath upon the children of men . . . ; wherefore he advocateth the cause of the children of men."[19] In the end, "the saints shall be filled with his glory, and receive their inheritance"[20] as "joint-heirs with Christ."[21]

Our desire is that these principles will help all have increased hope in Christ and feel a sense of belonging.

Never forget that you are a child of God, our Eternal Father, now and forever. He loves you, and the Church wants and needs you. Yes, we need you! We need your voices, talents, skills, goodness, and righteousness.

For many years, we have talked about "young single adults," "single adults," and "adults." Those designations can be administratively helpful *at times* but can inadvertently change how we perceive others.

Is there a way to avoid this human tendency that can separate us from one another?

President Nelson asked that we refer to ourselves as members of The Church of Jesus Christ of Latter-day Saints. That seems to cover all of us, doesn't it?

The gospel of Jesus Christ has the power to unite us. We are ultimately more alike than we are different. As members of God's family, we are truly brothers and sisters. Paul stated, "And [God] hath made of one blood all nations of men for to dwell on all the face of the earth."[22]

To you stake presidents, bishops, and quorum and sister leaders, I ask you to consider every member of your stake, ward, quorum, or organization as a member who can contribute and serve in callings and participate in many ways.

Every member in our quorums, organizations, wards, and stakes has God-given gifts and talents that can help build up His kingdom now.

Let us call upon our members who are single to serve, lift, and teach. Disregard old notions and ideas that have sometimes unintentionally contributed to their feelings of loneliness and that they do not belong or cannot serve.

I bear my witness on this Easter weekend of our Savior, Jesus Christ, and the eternal hope He gives me and all who believe in His name. And I bear this testimony humbly in His sacred name, even Jesus Christ, amen.

Notes

1. Matthew 11:28–30.
2. Matthew 11:27.
3. Jennifer Wickham, "Is Having a Sense of Belonging Important?," *Speaking of Health* (blog), Mayo Clinic Health System, Mar. 8, 2019, mayoclinichealthsystem.org.
4. John 16:33; emphasis added.
5. 1 Corinthians 15:3.
6. See John 20:19.

7. "The Family: A Proclamation to the World," ChurchofJesusChrist.org.
8. Doctrine and Covenants 76:79; see also Doctrine and Covenants 121:29.
9. Articles of Faith 1:3.
10. Russell M. Nelson, "Celestial Marriage," *Ensign* or *Liahona*, Nov. 2008, 94.
11. See Mosiah 2:41.
12. Dallin H. Oaks, "The Great Plan of Happiness," *Ensign*, Nov. 1993, 75.
13. See Hebrews 11:13; 2 Nephi 26:33; Alma 32:21; Ether 12:6; Articles of Faith 1:3.
14. See Isaiah 64:4; Doctrine and Covenants 133:45.
15. Mosiah 26:30.
16. See Alma 7:11–13.
17. Doctrine and Covenants 88:6.
18. John 16:33; see also Doctrine and Covenants 19:3.
19. Moroni 7:27–28.
20. Doctrine and Covenants 88:107.
21. Romans 8:17.
22. Acts 17:26.

PRIESTHOOD SESSION

APRIL 3, 2021

BISHOPS—SHEPHERDS OVER THE LORD'S FLOCK

ELDER QUENTIN L. COOK
Of the Quorum of the Twelve Apostles

My dear brethren of the priesthood, one of the most memorable lines in a much-loved hymn asks, "Shall the youth of Zion falter?"[1] My heartfelt and resounding declaration in answer to that question is "No!"

To make sure that answer holds true, I testify today that supporting the rising generation in a time of unusual challenges and temptations is an essential responsibility given to parents and bishoprics by Heavenly Father.[2] Let me illustrate the importance of a bishopric with a personal experience.

When I was a deacon, my family moved to a new home in a different ward. I was beginning junior high school, so I also attended a new school. There was a marvelous group of young men in the deacons quorum. Most of their parents were active members. My mother was completely active; my father was exceptional in every way but was not an active member.

The second counselor in the bishopric,[3] Brother Dean Eyre, was a devoted leader. When I was still adjusting to the new ward, a father-son event was announced for Bear Lake—about 40 miles (65 km) away. I did not think I would attend without my father. But Brother Eyre issued a special invitation for me to go with him. He spoke highly and respectfully of my father and stressed the significance of my opportunity to be with the other members of the deacons quorum. So I decided to go with Brother Eyre, and I had a wonderful experience.

Brother Eyre was a marvelous example of Christlike love in fulfilling the bishopric's responsibility to support parents in watching over and nurturing the youth. He gave me an excellent start in this new ward and was a mentor to me.

A few months before I left for a mission in 1960, Brother Eyre passed away from cancer at age 39. He left a wife and their five children, all younger than age 16. His oldest sons, Richard and Chris Eyre, have assured me that in the absence of their father, bishoprics supported and watched out for them and their younger brothers and sister with Christlike love, for which I am grateful.

Parents will always have the main responsibility for their families.[4] Quorum presidencies also provide essential support and guidance to quorum members by assisting them in elevating the duties and power of the Aaronic Priesthood to the center of their lives.[5]

Today my purpose is to focus on bishops and their counselors, who can appropriately be called "shepherds over the Lord's flock"— with emphasis on being shepherds for the rising generation.[6] It is interesting that the Apostle Peter referred to Jesus Christ as "the Shepherd and Bishop of your souls."[7]

The bishop has five principal responsibilities in presiding over a ward:

1. He is the presiding high priest in the ward.[8]
2. He is president of the Aaronic Priesthood.[9]
3. He is a common judge.[10]
4. He coordinates the work of salvation and exaltation, including caring for those in need.[11]
5. And he oversees records, finances, and the use of the meetinghouse.[12]

In his role as presiding high priest, the bishop is the ward's "spiritual leader."[13] He is a "faithful disciple of Jesus Christ."[14]

In addition, "the bishop coordinates the work of salvation and exaltation in the ward."[15] The bishop should assign the day-to-day responsibility for sharing the gospel, strengthening new and returning members, ministering, and temple and family history work to the elders quorum and Relief Society presidencies.[16] The bishop coordinates this work in the ward council and ward youth council.

The bishop has a paramount role in serving as a shepherd to guide the rising generation, including young single adults, to Jesus Christ.[17] President Russell M. Nelson has emphasized the seminal role of the bishop and his counselors. He has taught that their "first and foremost responsibility is to care for the young men and young women of [their] ward."[18] The bishopric supports parents in watching over and nurturing children and youth in the ward. The bishop and ward Young Women president counsel together. They strive to help the youth live the standards in *For the Strength of Youth*, qualify to receive ordinances, and make and keep sacred covenants.

You might ask, "Why is the bishop directed to spend so much time with the youth?" The Lord has organized His Church to accomplish crucial priorities. Accordingly, the organization of His Church has a structure in which the bishop has a dual responsibility. He has doctrinal responsibility for the ward as a whole, but he also has specific doctrinal responsibility for the priests quorum.[19]

The young men who are priests and the young women of the same age are at a very important stage in their lives and development. During a short period of time, they make decisions that have significant lifelong implications. They determine whether they will qualify for the temple, serve a mission,[20] strive to be married in the temple, and prepare for their life's work. These decisions, once made, have profound spiritual and practical implications for the remainder of their lives. Bishops, please know that a relatively short time spent with a young priest, young woman, or young adult can help them understand the power available to them through the Atonement of Jesus Christ. It can provide a vision that will have a profound influence upon their entire life.

One of the best examples I have seen of a bishop who helped provide this kind of vision for his youth was Bishop Moa Mahe. He was called to be the first bishop of the San Francisco Tongan Ward.[21] He was an immigrant from Vava'u, Tonga. His ward was located near the San Francisco, California, airport, where he worked.[22]

The ward had a large number of youth, most from families who had recently immigrated to the United States. Bishop Mahe not only taught them in word and by example how to be righteous disciples of Jesus Christ, but he also helped give them a vision of what they could become and helped them prepare for the temple, missions, education, and employment. He served for almost eight years, and his dreams and desires for the youth became a reality.

Nearly 90 percent of the young men in the Aaronic Priesthood quorums served missions. Fifteen young men and women were the first members of their families to attend college.[23] He met with the principal of the local high school (not of our faith), and they forged a friendship and collaborated on how to assist each young person to achieve worthwhile goals and overcome problems. The principal told me that Bishop Mahe assisted him in working with immigrants of all faiths who were struggling. The young people knew that the bishop loved them.

Sadly, Bishop Mahe passed away while serving as bishop. I will never forget his touching and inspiring funeral. There was a huge crowd. The choir was composed of more than 35 faithful young members who had served missions or were attending college and who had been youth during his service as bishop. One speaker expressed the intense feeling of appreciation from the youth and young adults in his ward. He paid tribute to Bishop Mahe for the vision he had given them in preparing for life and righteous service. But most important, Bishop Mahe had assisted them in building faith in the Lord Jesus Christ as the foundation of their lives.

Now, bishops, wherever you serve, in your interviews and other associations, you can provide that kind of vision and build faith in Jesus Christ. You can extend powerful invitations to change behavior, prepare them for life, and inspire them to stay on the covenant path.

In addition, you may help some youth who are in conflict with parents over things that are relatively unimportant.[24] At a time when young people seem to have maximum conflict with their parents, the person who presides over their quorum and to whom they answer ecclesiastically is also the person to whom their parents go for temple recommends. This puts the bishop in a unique position to counsel both the youth and their parents when contention has created a division. Bishops can help both view things with an eternal perspective and resolve issues of more or less importance. We recommend that bishops not have assigned ministering families so they can focus their time and energy ministering to the youth and their families in these kinds of situations.[25]

I am aware of one bishop who was able to resolve extreme contention between a son and his parents, bringing harmony to the home and enhanced commitment to the gospel. The bishop helped the parents understand that striving to be a disciple of Jesus Christ was more important than exactly how and when family chores were accomplished.

In order to spend more time with youth, wherever they are, including at school events or activities, bishoprics have been counseled to delegate appropriate meetings and counseling time with adults. While bishops can counsel on acute and urgent matters, we recommend that delegation of ongoing counseling with chronic, less urgent matters that do not involve judgments as to worthiness be assigned to members of the elders quorum or Relief Society—usually presidencies or ministering brothers and sisters. The Spirit will guide the leaders[26] to select the right members to undertake this counseling. Those who receive this delegated counseling assignment are entitled to revelation. They, of course, must always maintain strict confidentiality.

Thoughtful leaders have always sacrificed for the rising generation. This is where the bishopric members spend the majority of their Church-service time.

I now desire to say a few things directly to the youth and then to our bishops.

Many of you precious young people may not have a clear vision of who you are and who you can become. Yet you are at the threshold of the most important decisions you will make in your lives. Please counsel with both your parents and your bishop about important choices that are ahead of you. Allow the bishop to be your friend and counselor.

We are aware that you have trials and temptations coming at you from every direction. We all need to repent daily, as President Nelson has taught. Please talk to your bishop about any matter in which a common judge can assist you in getting your life in order with the Lord in preparation for the "great work" He has for you in this final dispensation.[27] As President Nelson has invited you, please qualify yourself to be part of the Lord's youth battalion![28]

Now a word for you precious bishops on behalf of the leadership and members of the Church. We express our deep gratitude to you. With the adjustments that you have been requested to make in recent years, dear bishops, please know how much we love and appreciate you. Your contribution to the kingdom is almost beyond description. The Church has 30,900 bishops and branch presidents serving across the world.[29] We honor each of you.

Some words and the sacred callings they describe are imbued with almost a spiritual, transcendent significance. The calling of *bishop* is definitely in the top tier of such words. To serve the Lord in this capacity is remarkable in so many ways. The calling, sustaining, and setting apart of a bishop is a never-to-be-forgotten experience. For me, it ranks with a small number of sublime events in the wide range and depth of feelings it evokes. It sits comfortably in a hierarchy of precious events like marriage and fatherhood that cannot be described in a few words.[30]

Bishops, we sustain you! Bishops, we love you! You are truly the Lord's shepherds over His flock. The Savior will not forsake you in these sacred callings. Of this I testify, on this Easter weekend, in the name of Jesus Christ, amen.

Notes

1. "True to the Faith," *Hymns*, no. 254.
2. Youth leaders, quorum and class presidencies, and other Church leaders share this responsibility.
3. The bishop is president of the priests quorum. His first counselor has responsibility for the teachers quorum, and his second counselor has responsibility for the deacons quorum. (See *General Handbook: Serving in The Church of Jesus Christ of Latter-day Saints*, 10.3, ChurchofJesusChrist .org.)
4. See Doctrine and Covenants 68:25–28.
5. See Quentin L. Cook, "Adjustments to Strengthen Youth," *Ensign* or *Liahona*, Nov. 2019, 40–43.
6. The use of the word *bishop* applies with equal force to our faithful branch presidents.
7. 1 Peter 2:25.
8. See *General Handbook*, 6.1.1.
9. See *General Handbook*, 6.1.2.
10. See *General Handbook*, 6.1.3.
11. See *General Handbook*, 6.1.4.

12. See *General Handbook*, 6.1.5.

13. *General Handbook*, 6.1.1; see also *General Handbook*, 6.1.1.1–6.1.1.4.

14. *General Handbook*, 6.1.1.

15. *General Handbook*, 6.1.4.

16. See *General Handbook*, 21.2; 23.5; 25.2.

17. See *General Handbook*, 6.1; 14.3.3.1; see also Quentin L. Cook, "Adjustments to Strengthen Youth," 40–43. The bishop has also been encouraged to spend more time with his wife and family. Such focus is made possible as capable adult advisers and specialists are called to assist the Aaronic Priesthood quorum presidencies and the bishopric in their duties.

18. Russell M. Nelson, "Witnesses, Aaronic Priesthood Quorums, and Young Women Classes," *Ensign* or *Liahona*, Nov. 2019, 39.

19. See Doctrine and Covenants 107:87–88.

20. "The Lord expects each able young man to prepare to serve [a mission] (see Doctrine and Covenants 36:1, 4–7). Young women and senior members who desire to serve should also prepare. An essential part of preparation is striving to become converted to Jesus Christ and His restored gospel. Those who desire to serve also prepare physically, mentally, emotionally, and financially" (*General Handbook*, 24.0).

21. The ward was organized on December 17, 1980. Elder John H. Groberg of the First Quorum of the Seventy helped organize this Tongan-language ward. (See Gordon Ashby, chairman, and Donna Osgood, ed., *The San Francisco California Stake: The First 60 Years, 1927–1987* [1987], 49–52.)

22. Bishop Mahe had advanced to a management position with Pan American Airways at the San Francisco, California, international airport.

23. See *The San Francisco California Stake*, 49.

24. They may also be rebelling against things that are eternally significant.

25. See *General Handbook*, 21.2.1.

26. The bishop will coordinate with the elders quorum and Relief Society presidencies with respect to who should be assigned and how loving and caring follow-up should be achieved.

27. Doctrine and Covenants 64:33.

28. See Russell M. Nelson, "Hope of Israel" (worldwide youth devotional, June 3, 2018), HopeofIsrael.ChurchofJesusChrist.org.

29. As of February 19, 2021, there were 24,035 bishops and 6,865 branch presidents serving throughout the world.

30. I was called as the bishop of the Burlingame Ward in California in 1974 by President David B. Barlow and set apart on September 15, 1974, by Elder Neal A. Maxwell, who had recently been called as an Assistant to the Quorum of the Twelve Apostles.

YOU CAN GATHER ISRAEL!

AHMAD S. CORBITT

First Counselor in the Young Men General Presidency

Almost three years ago, President Russell M. Nelson invited all youth of The Church of Jesus Christ of Latter-day Saints "to enlist in the Lord's youth battalion to help gather Israel" on both sides of the veil. He said, "That gathering is the most important thing taking place on earth today."[1] I am absolutely sure you youth can do this—and do it very well—because of (1) something about your identity and (2) an enormous power within you.

Forty-one years ago, two missionaries from our Church felt led to a house in New Jersey, in the United States. In time, miraculously, both parents and all 10 children were baptized. In the prophet's words, they "let God prevail"[2] in their lives. I should say "our lives." I was the third child. I was 17 years old when I decided to make a permanent covenant to follow Jesus Christ. But guess what else I decided? I would not serve a full-time mission. That was too much. And this could not be expected of me, right? I was a brand-new Church member. I had no money. Besides, although I had just graduated from the toughest high school in nearby West Philadelphia and faced down some dangerous challenges, I was secretly terrified of leaving home for two whole years.

Your True Identity

But I had just learned that I and all of humanity had lived with our Heavenly Father as His spirit sons and daughters before our birth. Others needed to know, as I knew, that He longed for all His children to enjoy eternal life with Him. So, before anyone was on earth, He presented all with His perfect plan of salvation and happiness, with Jesus Christ as our Savior. Tragically, Satan opposed God's plan.[3] According to the book of Revelation, "there was war in heaven"![4] Satan cunningly deceived a third part of Heavenly Father's spirit children into letting him prevail instead of God.[5] But not you!

The Apostle John saw that you overcame Satan "by the word of [your] testimony."[6]

Knowing my true identity, helped by my patriarchal blessing, gave me the courage and faith to accept President Spencer W. Kimball's invitation to gather Israel.[7] It will be the same for you, dear friends. Knowing you overcame Satan by the word of your testimony before will help you love, share, and invite[8] now and always—to invite others to come and see, come and help, and come and belong, as that same war for the souls of God's children rages on.

The Powerful Faith within You

What about the enormous power within you? Think of this: you shouted for joy[9] to come to a fallen world where all would face physical and spiritual death. We would never be able to overcome either on our own. We would suffer from not only our own sins but others' sins too. Humanity would experience virtually every imaginable type of brokenness and disappointment[10]—all with a veil of forgetfulness over our minds and the world's worst enemy continuing to target and tempt us. All hope for returning resurrected and clean to God's holy presence rested entirely upon one Being keeping His promise.[11]

What empowered you to go forward? President Henry B. Eyring taught, "It took faith in Jesus Christ to sustain the plan of happiness and Jesus Christ's place in it when you knew so little of the challenges that you would face in mortality."[12] When Jesus Christ promised He would come into mortality and give His life to gather[13] and save us, you did not simply believe Him. You "noble spirits"[14] had such "exceedingly great faith" that you saw His promise as sure.[15] He could not lie, so you saw Him as if He had already shed His blood for you, long before He was born.[16]

In John's symbolic words, you "overcame [Satan] by the blood of the Lamb."[17] President Dallin H. Oaks taught that in that world "[you] saw the end from the beginning."[18]

Suppose one day before you leave for school, one of your parents makes a true promise that you can have your favorite food when you return home! You are excited! While in school you imagine eating that food, and you can already taste it. Naturally, you share your good news with others. Looking forward to going home makes you so happy that the tests and challenges of school seem light. Nothing can take away your joy or make you doubt because of how sure the promise is! Similarly, before you noble spirits were born, you learned to see Christ's promises in this sure way, and you tasted of His salvation.[19] Your great faith is like muscles that get stronger and bigger the more you exercise them, but they are already inside you.

How can you awaken your giant faith in Christ and use it to gather Israel now and triumph over Satan again? By relearning to look forward and see with that same certainty the Lord's promise to gather and save today. He mainly uses the Book of Mormon and His prophets to teach us how. Long before Christ, the Nephite "prophets, and . . . priests, and . . . teachers . . . [persuaded the people] to look forward unto the Messiah, and believe in him to come as though he already was."[20] The prophet Abinadi taught, "And now if Christ had not come into the world, speaking of things to come as though they had already come, there could have been no redemption."[21] Like Alma, Abinadi "look[ed] forward with an eye of faith"[22] and saw God's sure promise of salvation as already fulfilled. They "overcame [Satan] by the blood of the Lamb, and . . . the word of their testimony" long before Christ was born, just as you did. And the Lord gave them power to invite and gather Israel. He will do the same for you as you look forward in faith, see Israel gathered—globally and in your own "circles"[23]—and invite all!

Hundreds of missionaries built upon their powerful premortal faith in Christ by envisioning those they contacted or taught dressed in baptismal and temple clothing. In a talk titled "Begin with the End in Mind,"[24] President Nelson shared a personal example of doing this and instructed mission leaders to teach our missionaries to do the same. Knowing they exercised this great faith in Jesus Christ in the premortal world immensely helped our dear missionaries "hear Him"[25] and activate their enormous faith to gather Israel as the Lord promised.

Of course, imagining lies harms faith.[26] My friends, intentionally envisioning or viewing things that conflict with who you really are, especially pornography, will weaken your faith in Christ and, without repentance, could destroy it. Please use your imaginations to increase faith in Christ, not ruin it.

The Children and Youth Program

The Children and Youth program is a prophetic tool to help you youth power up your great faith. President Oaks taught, "This program is designed to help you become more like our Savior in four areas: spiritual, social, physical, and intellectual."[27] As you youth lead—*lead*—in living the gospel, caring for others, inviting all to receive the gospel, uniting families for eternity, and organizing fun activities,[28] the great faith in Christ you had in the premortal life will resurface and empower you to do His work in this life!

Also, personal goals, "especially short-term goals,"[29] help you reignite your powerful faith. When you set a good goal, you are looking forward, as you did before, and seeing what your Heavenly Father wants you or another to become.[30] Then you plan and work hard to achieve it. Elder Quentin L. Cook taught, "Never underestimate the importance of planning, setting goals . . . , and [inviting others]—all with an eye of faith."[31]

The choice is yours! The Lord said of you, "The power [to choose] is in them."[32] Elder Neil L. Andersen explained, "Your faith will grow not by chance, but by choice."[33] He also said, "[Any] honest questions [you may have] . . . will be settled with patience and an eye of faith."[34]

I testify that (1) your true identity and (2) the enormous power of faith in Christ within you will enable you to "help prepare the world for the Savior's return by inviting all to come unto Christ and receive the blessings of His Atonement."[35] May we all share the joy of the Book of Mormon's sure promise:

"The righteous that hearken unto the . . . prophets, and . . . look forward unto Christ with steadfastness . . . notwithstanding all persecution . . . shall not perish.

"But [Christ] . . . shall heal them, and they shall have peace with him."[36]

In the name of Jesus Christ, amen.

Notes

1. Russell M. Nelson, "Hope of Israel" (worldwide youth devotional, June 3, 2018), HopeofIsrael.ChurchofJesusChrist.org.
2. See Russell M. Nelson, "Let God Prevail," *Ensign* or *Liahona*, Nov. 2020, 92–95.
3. See Gospel Topics, "Plan of Salvation," topics.ChurchofJesusChrist.org; see also Henry B. Eyring, "The Power of Sustaining Faith," *Ensign* or *Liahona*, May 2019, 58.
4. See Revelation 12:7–8.
5. See Doctrine and Covenants 29:36–37.
6. Revelation 12:11.
7. See Spencer W. Kimball, "It Becometh Every Man," *Ensign*, Oct. 1977, 2–7.
8. "Sharing the Gospel," ChurchofJesusChrist.org/share.
9. See Job 38:4–7.
10. See Gospel Topics, "Plan of Salvation"; see also "Be Still, My Soul," *Hymns*, no. 124, verse 3.
11. See Gospel Topics, "Plan of Salvation"; see also Dallin H. Oaks, "The Great Plan," *Ensign* or *Liahona*, May 2020, 93–94, 96.
12. Henry B. Eyring, "The Power of Sustaining Faith," 58.
13. See 3 Nephi 27:14.
14. Russell M. Nelson, "Hope of Israel," HopeofIsrael.ChurchofJesusChrist.org; see also Doctrine and Covenants 138:55–56.
15. See Alma 13:2–4; see also Revelation 12:11; Articles of Faith 1:5. The Book of Mormon makes clear that those with "exceedingly great faith" see God's promises as already fulfilled. See 1 Nephi 5:5; Mosiah 3:11–13; 4:1–3; Alma 27:28; 28:12 ("they *are* raised" in 77–76 BC; emphasis added); see also Exodus 3:13; Isaiah 53; Doctrine and Covenants 130:7; Moses 7:47.
16. See 2 Nephi 31:15; Ether 3:6–9, 11–13. Faith to see Christ's promise of salvation as already fulfilled necessarily requires knowing Christ cannot lie. Such faith is a defining characteristic of the premortal faithful, particularly our youth. "Our Heavenly Father has reserved many of His most noble spirits—perhaps, I might say, His finest team—for this final phase. Those noble spirits—those finest players, those heroes—are *you*!" (Russell M. Nelson, "Hope of Israel," HopeofIsrael.ChurchofJesusChrist.org). See also John 1:1; 14:6, 17.
17. Revelation 12:11; see also Ether 3:6–9.
18. Dallin H. Oaks, "The Great Plan," 93.
19. See Alma 36:24–26; see also Psalm 34:8; Jacob 3:2; Mosiah 4:11.
20. Jarom 1:11.
21. Mosiah 16:6.
22. Alma 5:15.
23. See "Gospel Living: Circles," *New Era*, Oct. 2020, 15.
24. See Russell M. Nelson, "Begin with the End in Mind" (address given at the seminar for new mission presidents, June 22, 2014).
25. See Russell M. Nelson, "Hear Him," *Ensign* or *Liahona*, May 2020, 88–92.
26. For example, Alma spoke to his people about looking forward with an eye of faith to when they would stand before God but warned they could not imagine doing so with confidence and peace unless they had repented of their sins (see Alma 5:15–17).
27. Face to Face with President and Sister Oaks (worldwide youth and children's broadcast, Feb. 23, 2020), facetoface.ChurchofJesusChrist.org.
28. See *General Handbook: Serving in The Church of Jesus Christ of Latter-day Saints*, 1.2; 10.2.1.3; 11.2.1.3, ChurchofJesusChrist.org.
29. Face to Face with President and Sister Oaks, facetoface.ChurchofJesusChrist.org.

30. See *Preach My Gospel: A Guide to Missionary Service* (2018), 156, ChurchofJesusChrist.org; see also Alma 5:15–17.
31. Quentin L. Cook, "Purpose and Planning" (address given at the seminar for new mission presidents, June 25, 2019).
32. Doctrine and Covenants 58:28.
33. Neil L. Andersen, "Faith Is Not by Chance, but by Choice," *Ensign* or *Liahona*, Nov. 2015, 66.
34. Neil L. Andersen, "The Eye of Faith," *Ensign* or *Liahona*, May 2019, 36.
35. "Aaronic Priesthood Quorum Theme," ChurchofJesusChrist.org.
36. 2 Nephi 26:8–9.

THIS IS OUR TIME!

ELDER S. GIFFORD NIELSEN

Of the Seventy

In 1978, I stood on a football field in a stadium packed with 65,000 fans. In front of me were several very large opponents who looked like they wanted to take my head off. It was my first game as a starting quarterback in the National Football League, and we were playing the reigning Super Bowl champions. To be honest, I questioned whether I was good enough to be on the field. I dropped back to throw my first pass, and as I released the ball, I was hit harder than I'd ever been hit before. At that moment, lying under a pile of those massive athletes, I wondered what I was doing there. I had a decision to make. Would I let my doubts overtake me, or would I find courage and strength to get up and to carry on?

I didn't realize at the time how this experience would prepare me for future opportunities. I needed to learn that I could be strong and courageous in the face of difficult situations.

A football game might not be nearly as important as the challenges you will face. In most cases, there won't be a stadium full of people watching. But your valiant decisions will have eternal significance.

Maybe we don't always feel up to the challenge. But our Heavenly Father sees us as fearless builders of His kingdom. That is why He sent us here during this most decisive time in the world's history. This is our time!

Listen to what President Russell M. Nelson said shortly after becoming President of the Church: "Our Savior and Redeemer, Jesus Christ, will perform some of His mightiest works between now and when He comes again. We will see miraculous indications that God the Father and His Son, Jesus Christ, preside over this Church in majesty and glory" ("Revelation for the Church, Revelation for Our Lives," *Ensign* or *Liahona*, May 2018, 96).

Mightiest works? Miraculous indications? What will that look like? What role will we play, and how will we understand what to do? I don't know all the answers, but I do know that the Lord needs us to be ready! Worthily exercising priesthood power has never been more crucial.

Do we believe God's prophet? Can we find and fulfill our destiny? Yes, we can, and yes, we must, because this is our time!

When we hear stories of God's mighty servants who came before us—like Moses, Mary, Moroni, Alma, Esther, Joseph, and many others—they seem bigger than life. But they were not that different from us. They were regular people who faced challenges. They trusted the Lord. They made the right choices at pivotal moments. And, with faith in Jesus Christ, they performed the works required in their time.

Consider the Old Testament hero Joshua. He was a devoted follower of Moses, one of the greatest leaders in history. After Moses departed, it was Joshua's time. He was to lead the children of Israel into the promised land. How would he do that? Joshua had been born and raised in slavery in Egypt. He had no handbook or instructional videos to help him. He didn't even have a smartphone! But he did have this promise from the Lord:

"As I was with Moses, so I will be with thee: I will not fail thee, nor forsake thee.

"Be strong and of a good courage" (Joshua 1:5–6).

When I was a new and inexperienced Seventy, I received an urgent phone call from the Office of the First Presidency, asking if I would represent the prophet in visiting a young man in the hospital—immediately. The young man's name was Zach. He was preparing to be a missionary but had been in an accident and suffered a serious head injury.

As I drove to the hospital, my mind raced. An errand for the prophet—are you kidding? What am I going to face? How will I help this young man? Do I have enough faith? Fervent prayer and the knowledge that I possessed the authority of the holy priesthood became my anchors.

When I arrived, Zach was lying in a hospital bed. An orderly stood ready to whisk him to the operating room so doctors could relieve the pressure on his brain. I looked at his tearful mom and a fearful young friend standing nearby, and I knew clearly that Zach needed a priesthood blessing. His friend had recently received the Melchizedek Priesthood, so I asked him to help me. I felt the power of the priesthood as we humbly gave Zach a blessing. Then he was hurried away for the surgery, and a peaceful feeling confirmed that the Savior would handle things according to His wisdom.

The medical staff performed one last X-ray before making the initial incision. They discovered, to their astonishment, that no operation would be needed.

After much therapy, Zach learned to walk and talk again. He served a successful mission and is now raising a beautiful family.

Of course, that is not always the outcome. I have given other priesthood blessings with equal faith, and the Lord did not grant complete healing in this life. We trust His purposes and leave the results to Him. We can't always choose the outcome of our actions, but we can choose to be ready to act.

You might not ever be asked by the First Presidency to represent them in a life-threatening situation. But we are all called upon to do life-changing things as representatives of the Lord. He will not forsake us. This is our time!

Peter, the Savior's chief Apostle, was in a ship on the sea when he saw Jesus walking on the water. He wanted to join Him, and the Savior said, "Come." Courageously and miraculously, Peter left the safety of the boat and began walking toward the Savior. But when Peter focused on the boisterous wind, his faith faltered. "He was afraid; and beginning to sink, he cried, saying, Lord, save me. And immediately Jesus stretched forth his hand, and caught him." (See Matthew 14:22–33.)

When winds blow in our lives, where is our focus? Remember, there is always one reliable source of strength and courage. The arms of Jesus extend to us, just as they extended to Peter. As we reach for Him, He will lovingly rescue us. We are His. He said, "Fear not: for I have redeemed thee, I have called thee by thy name; thou art mine" (Isaiah 43:1). He will prevail in your life if you let Him. The choice is yours. (See Russell M. Nelson, "Let God Prevail," *Ensign* or *Liahona*, Nov. 2020, 92–95.)

At the end of his life, Joshua pleaded with his people, "Choose you this day whom ye will serve; . . . but as for me and my house, we will serve the Lord" (Joshua 24:15). Because of the choices he made to serve the Lord, Joshua became a great leader in his time. My dear friends, this is our time! And the choices we make will determine our destiny (see Thomas S. Monson, "Decisions Determine Destiny" [Brigham Young University fireside, Nov. 6, 2005], speeches.byu.edu).

While I was serving as a bishop, we had a motto in our ward: Good choices equal happiness—eternally. The youth would pass me in the hall saying, "Bishop, I'm making good choices!" That's a bishop's dream!

What do we mean by "good choices"? Someone once asked Jesus, "Which is the great commandment in the law?" He answered:

"Thou shalt love the Lord thy God with all thy heart, and with all thy soul, and with all thy mind.

"This is the first and great commandment.

"And the second is like unto it, Thou shalt love thy neighbour as thyself" (Matthew 22:36–39).

I don't know about you, but when I read these two great commandments, I detect a third, implied commandment: to love thyself.

Have you ever thought of loving yourself as a commandment? Can we truly love God and love His children if we don't love ourselves?

A wise leader recently counseled a man who was trying to overcome years of destructive choices. The man felt ashamed, doubting that he was worthy of anyone's love.

His leader said to him, "The Lord knows you, loves you, and is pleased [with] you and the courageous steps you are taking." But then he added, "[You] need to hear the commandment to love yourself so you can feel [God's] love and love others."

When this brother heard that counsel, he saw life with new eyes. He later said, "I have spent my whole life trying to find peace and acceptance. I have looked for those things in many wrong places.

Only in the love of Heavenly Father and the Savior can I find comfort. I know They want me to love myself; it really is the only way I can feel Their love for me."

Our Heavenly Father wants us to love ourselves—not to become prideful or self-centered, but to see ourselves as He sees us: we are His cherished children. When this truth sinks deep into our hearts, our love for God grows. When we view ourselves with sincere respect, our hearts are open to treat others that way too. The more we recognize our divine worth, the better we understand this divine truth: that God has sent us right here, right now, at this momentous time in history, so that we can do the greatest possible good with the talents and gifts we have. This is our time! (See Russell M. Nelson, "Becoming True Millennials" [worldwide devotional for young adults, Jan. 10, 2016], broadcasts.ChurchofJesusChrist.org.)

Joseph Smith taught that every prophet in every age "looked forward with joyful anticipation to the day in which we live; . . . they have sung and written and prophesied of this our day; . . . we are the favored people that God has [chosen] to bring about the Latter-day glory" (*Teachings of Presidents of the Church: Joseph Smith* [2007], 186).

As you face your daily challenges, remember this reassurance offered by Elder Jeffrey R. Holland: "So much rests on our shoulders, but it will be a glorious and successful experience. . . . The victory in this final contest has already been declared. The victory is already in the record books . . . , the scriptures!" ("Be Not Afraid, Only Believe" [address to Church Educational System religious educators, Feb. 6, 2015], broadcasts.ChurchofJesusChrist.org).

On this beautiful Easter weekend, may I extend an invitation that we all pray to recognize and embrace our individual roles as we prepare for the glorious day when the Savior comes again. The Lord loves us more than we can comprehend, and He will answer our prayers! Whether we are on a football field, in a hospital room, or in any other place, we can be an important part of these remarkable events—because this is our time! In the name of Jesus Christ, amen.

BLESS IN HIS NAME

PRESIDENT HENRY B. EYRING

Second Counselor in the First Presidency

My dear brethren, fellow servants in the priesthood of God, it is an honor for me to speak to you tonight. You have my deepest respect and gratitude. When I speak with you and hear of your great faith, it is my belief that there is an ever-increasing priesthood power in the world, with ever stronger quorums and ever more faithful priesthood holders.

In my few moments this evening, I will speak to those of you who want to be *even more* effective in your personal priesthood service. You know of the charge that you are to magnify your call to serve.[1] But you may wonder what to magnify your calling can mean for you.

I will start with the newest deacons because they are the most likely to feel uncertain about what magnifying their priesthood service might mean. Newly ordained elders might also want to listen. And a bishop in his first weeks of service might be interested too.

It is instructive for me to look back on my days as a deacon. I wish that someone had told me then what I will suggest now. It could have helped in all the priesthood assignments that have come to me since then—even the ones I receive in the present day.

I was ordained a deacon in a branch so small that I was the only deacon and my brother Ted the only teacher. We were the only family in the branch. The entire branch met in our home. The priesthood leader for my brother and me was a new convert who had just received the priesthood himself. I believed then my only priesthood duty was to pass the sacrament in my own dining room.

When my family moved to Utah, I found myself in a large ward with many deacons. In my first sacrament meeting there, I observed the deacons—an army, it seemed to me—moving with precision as they passed the sacrament like a trained team.

I was so frightened that the next Sunday I went early to the ward building to be by myself when no one could see me. I remember that it was the Yalecrest Ward in Salt Lake City, and it had a statue on the grounds. I went behind the statue and prayed fervently for help to know how not to fail as I took my place in passing the sacrament. That prayer was answered.

But I know now that there is a better way to pray and to think as we try to grow in our priesthood service. It has come by my understanding why individuals are given the priesthood. The purpose for our receiving the priesthood is to allow us to bless people for the Lord, doing so in His name.[2]

It was years after I was a deacon when I learned what that means practically. For instance, as a high priest, I was assigned to visit a care center sacrament meeting. I was asked to pass the sacrament. Instead of thinking about the process or precision in the way I passed the sacrament, I instead looked in the faces of each elderly person. I saw many of them weeping. One lady grabbed my sleeve, looked up, and said aloud, "Oh, thank you, thank you."

The Lord had blessed my service given in His name. That day I had prayed for such a miracle to come instead of praying for how well I might do my part. I prayed that the people would feel the Lord's love through my loving service. I have learned this is the key to serving and blessing others in His name.

I heard a recent experience that reminded me of such love. When all Church meetings were suspended due to the COVID-19 pandemic, a ministering brother accepted an assignment from his elders quorum president to bless and administer the sacrament to a sister he ministers to. When he called her to offer to bring the sacrament, she accepted reluctantly, hating to take him out of his own home in such a dangerous time and also believing that things would quickly return to normal.

When he arrived at her home that Sunday morning, she had a request. Could they walk next door and also have the sacrament with her 87-year-old neighbor? With the bishop's authorization, he agreed.

For many, many weeks, and with very careful social distancing and other safety measures, that small group of Saints gathered each

Sunday for a simple sacrament service. Just a few pieces of broken bread and cups of water—but many tears shed for the goodness of a loving God.

In time, the ministering brother, his family, and the sister he ministers to were able to return to church. But the 87-year-old widow, the neighbor, out of an abundance of caution, had to remain home. The ministering brother—remember that his assignment was to her neighbor and not even to this elderly sister herself—still to this day quietly comes to her home each Sunday, scriptures and a tiny piece of bread in hand, to administer the sacrament of the Lord's Supper.

His priesthood service, like mine that day in the care center, is given out of love. In fact, the ministering brother recently asked his bishop if there were others in the ward he could care for. His desire to magnify his priesthood service has grown as he has served in the Lord's name and in a way known almost exclusively to Him. I don't know if the ministering brother has prayed, as I did, for those he serves to know of the Lord's love, but because his service has been in the Lord's name, the result has been the same.

The same wonderful result comes when I pray for it before I give a priesthood blessing to someone who is ill or in a time of need. It happened once in a hospital when impatient doctors urged me— more than urged me—*ordered me*—*t*o hurry and get out of the way so they could do their work, rather than giving me an opportunity to give the priesthood blessing. I stayed, and I did give the blessing. And that little girl I blessed that day, who the doctors had thought would die, lived. I am grateful at this moment that that day, I didn't let my own feelings get in the way but felt that the Lord wanted that little girl to have a blessing. And I knew what the blessing was: I blessed her to be healed. And she was.

It has happened many times as I have given a blessing to someone apparently near death, with family members surrounding the bed, hoping for a blessing of healing. Even if I have only a moment, I always pray to know what blessing the Lord has in store that I can give in His name. And I ask to know how He wants to bless that person and not what I or the people standing nearby want. My experience is that even when the blessing is not what the others desire for themselves or their loved ones, the Spirit touches hearts to experience acceptance and comfort rather than disappointment.

The same inspiration comes when patriarchs fast and pray for guidance to give the blessing the Lord wants for a person. Again, I have heard blessings given that surprised me and also surprised the person receiving the blessing. Clearly, the blessing was from the Lord—both the warnings it contains as well as the promises shared in His name. The patriarch's prayer and fasting were rewarded by the Lord.

As a bishop, I learned while conducting worthiness interviews to pray for the Lord to let me sense what He wanted for the person, keeping any inspiration He would provide unclouded by my own judgment. That is hard if the Lord, in love, may want to bless someone with correction. It takes effort to distinguish what the Lord wants from what you want and the other person may want.

I believe that we can magnify our priesthood service over our lifetime and perhaps beyond. It will depend on our diligence in trying to know the Lord's will and our efforts to hear His voice so that we can know better what He wants for the person we are serving for Him. That magnification will come in small steps. It may come slowly, but it will come. The Lord promises this to us:

"For whoso is faithful unto the obtaining these two priesthoods of which I have spoken, and the magnifying their calling, are sanctified by the Spirit unto the renewing of their bodies.

"They become the sons of Moses and of Aaron and the seed of Abraham, and the church and kingdom, and the elect of God.

"And also all they who receive this priesthood receive me, saith the Lord."[3]

It is my witness that the keys of the priesthood were restored to the Prophet Joseph Smith. Servants of the Lord appeared from heaven to restore the priesthood for the great events that have unfolded and that lie before us. Israel will be gathered. The Lord's people will be prepared for His glorious Second Coming. The

Restoration will continue. The Lord will reveal more of His will to His prophets and to His servants.

You may feel small compared to the great sweep of what the Lord will do. If you do, I invite you to ask prayerfully how the Lord sees you. He knows you personally, He conferred the priesthood upon you, and your rising up and magnifying the priesthood matter to Him because He loves you and He trusts you to bless people He loves in His name.

I bless you now to be able to feel His love and His trust, in the name of the Lord Jesus Christ, amen.

Notes

1. See Doctrine and Covenants 84:33.
2. See Doctrine and Covenants 132:47.
3. Doctrine and Covenants 84:33–35.

WHAT HAS OUR SAVIOR DONE FOR US?

PRESIDENT DALLIN H. OAKS

First Counselor in the First Presidency

In a Saturday evening meeting at a stake conference many years ago, I met a woman who said her friends had asked her to come back to church after many years of inactivity, but she could not think of any reason why she should. To encourage her, I said, "When you consider all of the things the Savior has done for you, you have many reasons to come back to worship and serve Him." I was astonished when she replied, "What's He done for me?"

What has Jesus Christ done for each of us? He has done everything that is essential for our journey through mortality toward the destiny outlined in the plan of our Heavenly Father. I will speak of four of the principal features of that plan. In each of these, His Only Begotten Son, Jesus Christ, is the central figure. Motivating all of this is "the love of God, which sheddeth itself abroad in the hearts of the children of men; wherefore, it is the most desirable above all things" (1 Nephi 11:22).

I.

Just before Easter Sunday, it is timely to speak first of the Resurrection of Jesus Christ. The Resurrection from the dead is the reassuring personal pillar of our faith. It adds meaning to our doctrine, motivation to our behavior, and hope for our future.

Because we believe the Bible and Book of Mormon descriptions of the literal Resurrection of Jesus Christ, we also accept the numerous scriptural teachings that a similar resurrection will come to all mortals who have ever lived upon this earth.[1] As Jesus taught, "Because I live, ye shall live also" (John 14:19). And His Apostle taught that "the dead shall be raised incorruptible" and "this mortal shall have put on immortality" (1 Corinthians 15:52, 54).

But the Resurrection gives us more than this assurance of immortality. It changes the way we view mortal life.

The Resurrection gives us the perspective and the strength to endure the mortal challenges faced by each of us and those we love. It gives us a new way to view the physical, mental, or emotional deficiencies we have at birth or acquire during mortal life. It gives us the strength to endure sorrows, failures, and frustrations. Because each of us has an assured resurrection, we know that these mortal deficiencies and oppositions are only temporary.

The Resurrection also gives us a powerful incentive to keep the commandments of God during our mortal lives. When we rise from the dead and proceed to our prophesied Final Judgment, we want to have qualified for the choicest blessings promised to resurrected beings.[2]

In addition, the promise that the Resurrection can include an opportunity to be with our family members—husband, wife, children, parents, and posterity—is a powerful encouragement to fulfill our family responsibilities in mortality. It also helps us live together in love in this life, and it comforts us in the death of our loved ones. We know that these mortal separations are only temporary, and we anticipate future joyful reunions and associations. The Resurrection provides us hope and the strength to be patient as we wait. It also prepares us with the courage and dignity to face our own death— even a death that might be called premature.

All of these effects of the Resurrection are part of the first answer to the question "What has Jesus Christ done for me?"

II.

For most of us, the opportunity to be forgiven of our sins is the major meaning of the Atonement of Jesus Christ. In worship, we reverently sing:

> *His precious blood he freely spilt;*
> *His life he freely gave,*
> *A sinless sacrifice for guilt,*
> *A dying world to save.*[3]

Our Savior and Redeemer endured incomprehensible suffering to become a sacrifice for the sins of all mortals who would repent.

This atoning sacrifice offered the ultimate good, the pure lamb without blemish, for the ultimate measure of evil, the sins of the entire world. It opened the door for each of us to be cleansed of our personal sins so we can be readmitted to the presence of God, our Eternal Father. This open door is available to all of the children of God. In worship, we sing:

> *I marvel that he would descend from his throne divine*
> *To rescue a soul so rebellious and proud as mine,*
> *That he should extend his great love unto such as I.*[4]

The magnificent and incomprehensible effect of the Atonement of Jesus Christ is based on God's love for each of us. It affirms His declaration that "the worth of souls"—every one—"is great in the sight of God" (Doctrine and Covenants 18:10). In the Bible, Jesus Christ explained this in terms of our Heavenly Father's love: "For God so loved the world, that he gave his only begotten Son, that whosoever believeth in him should not perish, but have everlasting life" (John 3:16). In modern revelation, our Redeemer, Jesus Christ, declared that *He* "so loved the world that he gave his own life, that as many as would believe might become the sons of God" (Doctrine and Covenants 34:3).

Is it any wonder, then, that the Book of Mormon: Another Testament of Jesus Christ concludes with the teaching that to become "perfect" and "sanctified in Christ," *we* must "love God with all [our] might, mind and strength"? (Moroni 10:32–33). His plan motivated by love must be received with love.

III.

What else has our Savior, Jesus Christ, done for us? Through the teachings of His prophets and through His personal ministry, Jesus taught us the plan of salvation. This plan includes the Creation, the purpose of life, the necessity of opposition, and the gift of agency. He also taught us the commandments and covenants we must obey and the ordinances we must experience to take us back to our heavenly parents.

In the Bible, we read His teaching: "I am the light of the world: he that followeth me shall not walk in darkness, but shall have the light of life" (John 8:12). And in modern revelation, we read, "Behold, I am Jesus Christ, . . . a light which cannot be hid in darkness" (Doctrine and Covenants 14:9). If we follow His teachings, He lights our path in this life and assures our destiny in the next.

Because He loves us, He challenges us to focus on Him instead of the things of this mortal world. In His great sermon on the bread of life, Jesus taught that we should not be among those who are most attracted to the things of the world—the things that sustain life on earth but give no nourishment toward eternal life.[5] As Jesus invited us again and again and again, "Follow me."[6]

IV.

Finally, the Book of Mormon teaches that as part of His Atonement, Jesus Christ "suffer[ed] pains and afflictions and temptations of every kind; and this that the word might be fulfilled which saith he will take upon him the pains and the sicknesses of his people" (Alma 7:11).

Why did our Savior suffer these mortal challenges "of every kind"? Alma explained, "And he will take upon him their infirmities, that his bowels may be filled with mercy, according to the flesh, that he may know according to the flesh how to succor [which means to give relief or aid to] his people according to their infirmities" (Alma 7:12).

Our Savior feels and knows our temptations, our struggles, our heartaches, and our sufferings, for He willingly experienced them all as part of His Atonement. Other scriptures affirm this. The New Testament declares, "In that he himself hath suffered being tempted, he is able to succour them that are tempted" (Hebrews 2:18). Isaiah teaches, "Fear thou not; for I am with thee: . . . I will strengthen thee; yea, I will help thee" (Isaiah 41:10). All who suffer any kind of mortal infirmities should remember that our Savior experienced that kind of pain also, and that through His Atonement, He offers each of us the strength to bear it.

The Prophet Joseph Smith summarized all of this in our third article of faith: "We believe that through the Atonement of Christ, all mankind may be saved, by obedience to the laws and ordinances of the Gospel."

"What has Jesus Christ done for me?" that sister asked. Under the plan of our Heavenly Father, He "created the heavens and the earth" (Doctrine and Covenants 14:9) so that each of us could have the mortal experience necessary to seek our divine destiny. As part of the Father's plan, the Resurrection of Jesus Christ overcame death to assure each of us immortality. Jesus Christ's atoning sacrifice gives each of us the opportunity to repent of our sins and return clean to our heavenly home. His commandments and covenants show us the way, and His priesthood gives the authority to perform the ordinances that are essential to reach that destiny. And our Savior willingly experienced all mortal pains and infirmities that He would know how to strengthen us in our afflictions.

Jesus Christ did all of this because He loves all of the children of God. Love is the motivation for it all, and it was so from the very beginning. God has told us in modern revelation that "he created . . . male and female, after his own image . . . ; and gave unto them commandments that they should love and serve him" (Doctrine and Covenants 20:18–19).

I testify of all of this and pray that we all will remember what our Savior has done for each of us and that we all will love and serve Him, in the name of Jesus Christ, amen.

Notes

1. See, for example, 1 Corinthians 15:19–22; Helaman 14:17; Mormon 9:13.
2. See Alma 41.
3. "How Great the Wisdom and the Love," *Hymns*, no. 195, verse 2.
4. "I Stand All Amazed," *Hymns*, no. 193, verse 2.
5. See John 6:58.
6. See Topical Guide, "Follow."

WHAT WE ARE LEARNING AND WILL NEVER FORGET

PRESIDENT RUSSELL M. NELSON

President of The Church of Jesus Christ of Latter-day Saints

My dear brethren, I have looked forward to this virtual meeting with you. The last time we held a priesthood session of general conference was in April 2019. Much has happened in the past two years! Some of you have lost loved ones. Others have lost jobs, livelihood, or health. Still others have lost a sense of peace or hope for the future. My heart goes out to each one of you who has suffered these or other losses. I pray constantly that the Lord will comfort you. As you continue to let God prevail in your life, I know that He is just as optimistic about your future as He has ever been.

Amid the *losses* we have experienced, there are also some things we have *found*. Some have found deeper faith in our Heavenly Father and His Son, Jesus Christ. Many have found a fresh perspective on life—even an eternal perspective. You may have found stronger relationships with your loved ones and with the Lord. I hope you have found an increased ability to *hear Him* and receive personal revelation. Difficult trials often provide opportunities to grow that would not have come in any other way.

Think back on the past two years. How have you grown? What have you learned? You might initially wish you could go back to 2019 and stay there! But if you look at your life prayerfully, I believe you will see many ways in which the Lord has been guiding you through this time of hardship, helping you to become a more devoted, more converted man—a true man of God.

I know the Lord has great and marvelous plans for us—individually and collectively. With compassion and patience, He says:

"Ye are little children, and ye have not as yet understood how great blessings the Father hath . . . prepared for you;

"And ye cannot bear all things now; nevertheless, be of good cheer, for I will lead you along."[1]

My dear brothers, I testify that He has been, and *is,* indeed leading us along, as we seek to hear Him. He wants us to grow and to learn, even through—perhaps *especially* through—adversity.

Adversity is a great teacher. What have *you* learned in the past two years that you always want to remember? Your answers will be unique to you, but may I suggest four lessons I hope we have all learned and will never forget.

Lesson 1: The Home Is the Center of Faith and Worship

Often when the Lord warns us about the perils of the last days, He counsels thus: "Stand ye in holy places, and be not moved."[2] These "holy places" certainly include the Lord's temples and meetinghouses. But as our ability to gather in these places has been restricted in varying degrees, we have learned that one of the holiest of places on earth is the home—yes, even *your* home.

Brethren, you bear the priesthood of God. "The rights of the priesthood are inseparably connected with the powers of heaven."[3] You and your family have received priesthood ordinances. It is "in the ordinances [of the priesthood that] the power of godliness is manifest."[4] That power is available to you and your family *in your own home* as you keep the covenants you have made.[5]

Just 185 years ago, this very day, April 3, 1836, Elijah restored the keys of the priesthood that allow our families to be sealed together forever. That is why it felt so good to administer the sacrament in your home. How do you think it affected your family members to see you—their father, grandfather, husband, son, or brother—administer this holy ordinance? What will you do to retain that sacred feeling in your family?

You may feel that there is still more you need to do to make your home truly a sanctuary of faith. If so, please do it! If you are married, counsel with your wife as your equal partner in this crucial work. There are few pursuits more important than this. Between now and the time the Lord comes again, we all need our homes to be places of serenity and security.[6]

Attitudes and actions that invite the Spirit will increase the holiness of your home. Equally certain is the fact that *holiness will vanish* if there is anything in your behavior or environment that offends the Holy Spirit, for then "the heavens withdraw themselves."[7]

Have you ever wondered why the Lord wants us to make our homes the center of gospel learning and gospel living? It is not just to prepare us for, and help us through, a pandemic. Present restrictions on gathering will eventually end. However, your commitment to make your home your *primary* sanctuary of faith should *never* end. As faith and holiness decrease in this fallen world, your need for holy places will increase. I urge you to continue to make your home a truly holy place "and *be not moved*"[8] from that essential goal.

Lesson 2: We Need Each Other

God wants us to work together and help each other. That is why He sends us to earth in families and organizes us into wards and stakes. That is why He asks us to serve and minister to each other. That is why He asks us to live *in* the world but not be *of* the world.[9] We can accomplish so much more together than we can alone.[10] God's plan of happiness would be frustrated if His children remained isolated one from another.

The recent pandemic has been unique in that it has affected everyone in the world at essentially the same time. While some have suffered more than others, we have all been challenged in some way. Because of this, our common trial has the potential to help unite God's children as never before. So, I ask, has this shared trial drawn you closer to your neighbors—to your brothers and sisters across the street and around the world?

In this regard, the two great commandments can guide us: first, to love God and, second, to love our neighbor.[11] We show our love by serving.

If you know of anyone who is alone, reach out—even if you feel alone too! You do not need to have a reason or a message or business to transact. Just say hello and show your love. Technology can help you. Pandemic or not, each precious child of God needs to know that he or she is not alone!

Lesson 3: Your Priesthood Quorum Is
Meant for More Than Just a Meeting

During the pandemic, Sunday quorum meetings were canceled for a time. Some quorums are now able to meet virtually. Nevertheless, the work that the Lord has given to priesthood quorums was never meant to be confined to a meeting. Meetings are only a small part of what a quorum is meant for and what it can do.

My brethren of the Aaronic Priesthood and elders quorums, expand your vision of why we have quorums. How does the Lord wish you would use your quorum to accomplish His work—now? Seek revelation from the Lord. Humble yourself! Ask! Listen! If you have been called to lead, counsel as a presidency and with quorum members. Whatever your priesthood office or calling, let God prevail in your commitment as a member of your quorum and in your service. Experience with joy the righteousness you will bring to pass as you are "anxiously engaged in a good cause."[12] Quorums are in a unique position to accelerate the gathering of Israel on both sides of the veil.

Lesson 4: We Hear Jesus Christ
Better When We Are Still

We live in a time prophesied long ago, when "all things shall be in commotion; and surely, men's hearts shall fail them; for fear shall come upon all people."[13] That was true before the pandemic, and it will be true after. Commotion in the world will continue to increase. In contrast, the voice of the Lord is not "a voice of a great tumultuous noise, but . . . it [is] a still voice of perfect mildness, [like] a whisper, and it [pierces] even to the very soul."[14] In order to hear this still voice, you too must be still![15]

For a time, the pandemic has canceled activities that would normally fill our lives. Soon we may be able to choose to fill that time again with the noise and commotion of the world. Or we can use our time to hear the voice of the Lord whispering His guidance, comfort, and peace. Quiet time is sacred time—time that will facilitate personal revelation and instill peace.

Discipline yourself to have time alone and with your loved ones.

Open your heart to God in prayer. Take time to immerse yourself in the scriptures and worship in the temple.

My dear brethren, there are many things the Lord wants us to learn from our experiences during this pandemic. I have listed only four. I invite you to make your own list, consider it carefully, and share it with those you love.

The future is bright for God's covenant-keeping people.[16] The Lord will increasingly call upon His servants who worthily hold the priesthood to bless, comfort, and strengthen mankind and to help prepare the world and its people for His Second Coming. It behooves each of us to measure up to the sacred ordination we have received. We can do this! I so testify, with my expression of love for each of you, my beloved brethren, in the sacred name of Jesus Christ, amen.

Notes

1. Doctrine and Covenants 78:17–18.
2. Doctrine and Covenants 87:8; see also Matthew 24:15; Doctrine and Covenants 45:31–33; 101:21–22.
3. Doctrine and Covenants 121:36.
4. Doctrine and Covenants 84:20.
5. See John 4:20–23; Alma 32:9–16.
6. See Alma 50:4.
7. Doctrine and Covenants 121:37.
8. Doctrine and Covenants 87:8; emphasis added.
9. See John 17:15–16.
10. As an example, in 2020, the Church made donations to support more than 1,000 COVID-19 relief efforts around the globe. These efforts were made far more effective because we partnered with other humanitarian organizations, including Convoy of Hope, Feeding America, Partnership with Native Americans, the Salvation Army, the United Way, and the World Food Programme (see "2020 Year in Review," Newsroom, Dec. 21, 2020, newsroom .ChurchofJesusChrist.org). We extend our reach and our influence for good by working together.
11. See Mark 12:30–31.
12. See Doctrine and Covenants 58:27–28.
13. Doctrine and Covenants 88:91.
14. Helaman 5:30; see also 1 Kings 19:12; 3 Nephi 11:3.
15. See Psalm 46:10; Doctrine and Covenants 101:16.
16. See Doctrine and Covenants 82:14.

SUNDAY MORNING SESSION

APRIL 4, 2021

JESUS CHRIST: THE CAREGIVER OF OUR SOUL

ELDER ULISSES SOARES
Of the Quorum of the Twelve Apostles

My dear brothers and sisters, on this radiant Easter morning my heart rejoices upon remembering the most marvelous, the most majestic, the most immeasurable act that has occurred in all of human history—the atoning sacrifice of our Lord, Jesus Christ. The eminent words of the prophet Isaiah magnify the greatness and selflessness of the Savior's condescension and sacrifice in behalf of all the children of God:

"Surely he hath borne our griefs, and carried our sorrows: yet we did esteem him stricken, smitten of God, and afflicted.

"But he was wounded for our transgressions, he was bruised for our iniquities: the chastisement of our peace was upon him; and with his stripes we are healed."[1]

By voluntarily taking upon Himself the sins of all mankind, being cruelly nailed to the cross, and victoriously conquering death on the third day,[2] Jesus gave a more sacred significance to the Passover ordinance that had been bestowed upon Israel in ancient times.[3] In fulfillment of prophecy, He offered His own body and precious blood as the great and last sacrifice,[4] validating the traditional symbols used in the celebration of the Lord's Passover.[5] In so doing, Christ experienced physical and spiritual suffering that is incomprehensible to the human mind. The Savior Himself said:

"For behold, I, God, have suffered these things for all, . . .

"Which suffering caused myself, even God, the greatest of all, to tremble because of pain, and to bleed at every pore, and to suffer both body and spirit—and would that I might not drink the bitter cup, and shrink—

"Nevertheless, glory be to the Father, and I partook and finished my preparations unto the children of men."[6]

Christ graciously fulfilled the will of the Father[7] through His infinite and merciful sacrifice. He overcame the sting of physical and spiritual death,[8] introduced to the world through the Fall,[9] offering us the glorious possibility of eternal salvation.[10]

Jesus was the only Being capable of realizing this eternal and perfect sacrifice for all of us.[11] He was chosen and foreordained in the Grand Council in Heaven, even before the world was formed.[12] Furthermore, being born of a mortal mother, He inherited the physical death, but from God, as the Only Begotten Son of the Father, He inherited the power to lay down His own life and then to take it up again.[13] Additionally, Christ lived a perfect life that was without blemish and, therefore, was exempt from the demands of divine justice.[14] On some occasions the Prophet Joseph Smith taught:

"Salvation could not come to the world without the mediation of Jesus Christ.

"God . . . prepared a sacrifice in the gift of His own Son, who should be sent in due time to . . . open a door through which man might enter into the Lord's presence."[15]

While through His sacrifice the Savior unconditionally removed the effects of physical death,[16] He did not eliminate our personal responsibility to repent for the sins we commit.[17] Rather, He extended to us a loving invitation to be reconciled to our Eternal Father. Through Jesus Christ and His atoning sacrifice, we can experience a mighty change of mind and heart, bringing a fresh attitude, both toward God and toward life in general.[18] When we sincerely repent of our sins and turn our hearts and will to God and His commandments, we can receive His forgiveness and feel the influence of His Holy Spirit in greater abundance. Mercifully, we avoid having to experience the depth of suffering the Savior endured.[19]

The gift of repentance is an expression of God's kindness toward His children, and it is a demonstration of His incomparable power to help us overcome the sins we commit. It is also an evidence of the patience and long-suffering our loving Father has for our mortal weakness and frailties. President Russell M. Nelson, our beloved prophet, referred to this gift as "the key to happiness and peace of mind."[20]

My dear friends, I testify to you that as we genuinely repent of our sins,[21] we allow the atoning sacrifice of Christ to become wholly effective in our life.[22] We will become free from the bondage of sin, find joy in our earthly journey, and become eligible to receive eternal salvation, which was prepared from the foundation of the world for all who believe in Jesus Christ and come unto Him.[23]

In addition to providing the majestic gift of salvation, the Savior offers us relief and comfort as we face our afflictions, temptations, and weaknesses of mortal life, including the circumstances we have experienced recently in the current pandemic. I can assure you that Christ is ever aware of the adversities we experience in mortality. He understands all of the bitterness, agony, and physical pain as well as the emotional and spiritual challenges we face. The Savior's bowels are filled with mercy, and He is always ready to succor us. This is possible because He personally experienced and took upon Himself in the flesh the pain of our weakness and infirmities.[24]

With meekness and humility of heart, He descended below all things and accepted being despised, rejected, and humiliated by men, having been wounded for our transgressions and iniquities. He suffered these things for all, taking upon Himself the sins of the world,[25] thus becoming our ultimate spiritual caregiver.

As we draw nearer to Him, surrendering ourselves spiritually to His care, we will be able to take upon ourselves His yoke, which is easy, and His burden, which is light, thus finding that promised comfort and rest. Furthermore, we will receive the strength we all need to overcome the hardships, weaknesses, and sorrows of life, which are exceedingly difficult to endure without His help and healing power.[26] The scriptures teach us to "cast thy burden upon the Lord, and he shall sustain thee."[27] "And then may God grant unto [us] that [our] burdens may be light, through the joy of his Son."[28]

Near the end of last year, I learned of the passing of a dear couple, Mario and Regina Emerick, who were very faithful to the Lord and passed away four days apart from one another due to complications from COVID-19.

One of their sons, who is currently serving as a bishop in Brazil, related the following to me: "It was so difficult to see my parents depart from this world in that condition, but I could clearly feel the hand of the Lord in my life amidst that tragedy, because I received strength and peace that transcended my understanding. Through my faith in Jesus Christ and His Atonement, I received divine help to strengthen and comfort my family members and all those who helped us during this trying experience. Even though the miracle that everyone hoped for did not occur, personally I am a witness of many other miracles that have occurred in my own life and in the lives of my family members. I felt an inexplicable peace that penetrated the depths of my heart, giving me hope and confidence in the love of the Savior for me and in the plan of happiness of God for His children. I learned that on the very most grief-filled days, the loving arms of the Savior are always extended when we seek Him with all our heart, power, mind, and strength."

My dear brothers and sisters, on this Easter Sunday, I bear my solemn witness that Jesus rose from the dead and that He lives. I testify to you that through Him and His infinite Atonement, the Savior provided us the way to overcome death, both physically and spiritually. In addition to these great blessings, He also offers us comfort and assurance in difficult times. I assure you that as we put our trust in Jesus Christ and in His supernal atoning sacrifice, enduring in our faith to the end, we will enjoy the promises of our beloved Heavenly Father, who does everything within His power to help us return to His presence one day. This is His work and His glory![29] I testify to you that Jesus is the Christ, the Redeemer of the world, the promised Messiah, the Resurrection and the Life.[30] And I share these truths with you in His holy name, the Only Begotten of the Father, our Lord, Jesus Christ, amen.

Notes

1. Isaiah 53:4–5.
2. See Isaiah 53:7; 1 Nephi 11:21, 33; 13:40; Mosiah 14:7.
3. See Exodus 12–13, particularly Exodus 12:21, 43.
4. See Alma 34:14.
5. Elements of Passover that pointed to the Atonement of Jesus Christ included a sacrificial lamb (see Exodus 12:3, 5, 21), partaking of unleavened bread with bitter herbs (see Exodus 12:8, 15; Leviticus 23:6; Numbers 9:11), blood of the sacrificial lamb being placed on doorposts of homes (see Exodus 12:7, 13, 22–23), and the feast being eaten in haste (see Exodus 12:11).
6. Doctrine and Covenants 19:16, 18–19.

7. See John 6:38–40; 3 Nephi 27:13–15.

8. See 1 Corinthians 15:55–56; 2 Nephi 9:6–24; Mosiah 16:7–8; Alma 22:14.

9. See 2 Nephi 2:22; Moses 6:48.

10. See Alma 11:40; Doctrine and Covenants 76:41–42.

11. See Hebrews 5:9; Alma 34:9–10.

12. See Ether 3:14; Moses 4:1–2; Abraham 3:27.

13. See John 10:17–18.

14. See 1 Peter 1:19; 2 Nephi 2:7; Mosiah 15:2–5; see also Guide to the Scriptures, "Justice," scriptures .ChurchofJesusChrist.org.

15. *Teachings of Presidents of the Church: Joseph Smith* (2007), 48.

16. See Mosiah 15:8, 20; Alma 11:42–44; 40:23.

17. See John 3:16; Acts 17:30; Mosiah 2:41; Alma 42:6–9; 3 Nephi 11:31–40; Doctrine and Covenants 29:40–42; 133:16.

18. See Alma 5:13; see also Guide to the Scriptures, "Repent, Repentance," scriptures.Church ofJesusChrist.org.

19. See Alma 36:17–20; Doctrine and Covenants 19:4, 15–18.

20. Russell M. Nelson, "We Can Do Better and Be Better," *Ensign* or *Liahona*, May 2019, 67; see also 2 Nephi 9:23; Mosiah 4:6.

21. See 2 Nephi 10:24; Mosiah 5:1–2.

22. See Mosiah 26:29; 3 Nephi 9:20, 22; Moroni 6:8.

23. See Mosiah 2:41; Doctrine and Covenants 66:12; 75:5; 93:1.

24. See Hebrews 2:18; 4:15; Alma 7:11–13; Doctrine and Covenants 62:1.

25. See Isaiah 53:3–5; Alma 7:11–13; Doctrine and Covenants 88:6.

26. See Matthew 11:28–30; 2 Nephi 25:23; see also Ether 12:27.

27. Psalm 55:22.

28. Alma 33:23.

29. See Moses 1:39.

30. See John 11:25.

THE GRAVE HAS NO VICTORY

REYNA I. ABURTO

Second Counselor in the Relief Society General Presidency

On this glorious Easter Sunday, our children joyfully sing, "On a golden springtime, Jesus Christ awoke and left the tomb where he had lain; the bands of death he broke."[1]

We are grateful for our knowledge of the Resurrection of Jesus Christ. And yet at some point in our lives, we will have felt heartbroken after losing someone whom we love dearly. Through the current global pandemic, many of us have lost loved ones—either family members or friends.[2] We pray for those who are grieving such loss.

President Russell M. Nelson has said:

"Irrespective of age, we mourn for those loved and lost. Mourning is one of the deepest expressions of pure love. . . .

"Moreover, we can't fully appreciate joyful reunions later without tearful separations now. The only way to take sorrow out of death is to take love out of life."[3]

We can imagine how Jesus's friends, who had followed Him and ministered to Him,[4] felt upon witnessing His death.[5] We know that "they mourned and wept."[6] On the day of the Crucifixion, not knowing what would happen on Sunday, they must have been overwhelmed by distress, wondering how they would go on without their Lord. Nevertheless, they continued ministering to Him even in death.

Joseph of Arimathea begged Pilate to give him Jesus's body. He took the body down, wrapped it in fine linen, laid it in his own new tomb, and rolled a great stone to the door of the sepulchre.[7]

Nicodemus brought myrrh and aloes. He helped Joseph take the body and wrap it in linen with the spices.[8]

Mary Magdalene and other women followed Joseph and Nicodemus, watched where they laid Jesus's body, and prepared sweet spices and ointments to anoint it.[9] According to the strict laws of that day, they waited to further prepare and anoint the body because Saturday was the Sabbath.[10] Then, early in the morning on

Sunday, they went to the sepulchre. After realizing that the body of the Savior was not there, they went to tell the disciples who were Jesus's Apostles. The Apostles came with them to the tomb and saw that it was empty. All but Mary Magdalene eventually left, wondering what had happened to the Savior's body.[11]

Mary Magdalene stayed at the tomb by herself. Only a few days before, she had seen the tragic death of her friend and Master. Now His tomb was empty, and she did not know where He was. It was too much for her to take in, and she wept. At that moment, the resurrected Savior came to her and asked why she was weeping and whom she was seeking. Thinking that the gardener spoke to her, she asked that, if he had taken her Lord's body, to tell her where it was so she could get it.[12]

I imagine that the Lord may have allowed Mary Magdalene to grieve and to express her pain.[13] He then called her by her name, and she turned to Him and recognized Him. She saw the resurrected Christ and was a witness of His glorious Resurrection.[14]

Like you, in some way I can relate to the anguish felt by Mary Magdalene and her friends as they grieved the death of their Lord. When I was nine years old, I lost my older brother during a devastating earthquake. Because it happened unexpectedly, it took me a while to grasp the reality of what had occurred. I was heartbroken by sorrow, and I would ask myself, "What happened to my brother? Where is he? Where did he go? Will I ever see him again?"

Back then I did not yet know about God's plan of salvation, and I had the desire to know where we come from, what the purpose of life is, and what happens to us after we die. Don't we all have those yearnings when we lose a loved one or when we go through difficulties in our lives?

A few years after, I started thinking of my brother in a specific way. I would imagine him knocking on our door. I would open the door, he would be standing there, and he would tell me, "I am not dead. I am alive. I could not come to you, but now I will stay with you and never leave again." That imagining, almost a dream, helped me cope with the pain that I felt over losing him. The thought that he would be with me came to my mind over and over. Sometimes I would even stare at the door, hoping that he would knock and I would see him again.

About 40 years later, during Easter time, I was pondering about the Resurrection of Jesus Christ and started thinking about my brother. At that moment, something clicked in my mind. I remembered imagining him coming to see me.

That day I realized that the Spirit had given me comfort in a difficult time. I had received a witness that my brother's spirit is not dead; he is alive. He is still progressing in his eternal existence. I now know that "[my] brother shall rise again"[15] at that magnificent moment when, because of Jesus Christ's Resurrection, we will all be resurrected. In addition, He has made it possible for all of us to be reunited as families and have eternal joy in the presence of God if we will choose to make and keep sacred covenants with Him.

President Nelson has taught:

"Death is a necessary component of our eternal existence. No one knows when it will come, but it is essential to God's great plan of happiness. Thanks to the Atonement of the Lord, eventual resurrection is a reality and eternal life is a possibility for all humankind. . . .

". . . For sorrowing loved ones left behind . . . the sting of death is soothed by a steadfast faith in Christ, a perfect brightness of hope, a love of God and of all men, and a deep desire to serve them. That faith, that hope, that love will qualify us to come into God's holy presence and, with our eternal companions and families, dwell with Him forever."[16]

I testify that "if Christ had not risen from the dead, or have broken the bands of death that the grave should have no victory, and that death should have no sting, there could have been no resurrection.

"But there is a resurrection, therefore the grave hath no victory, and the sting of death is swallowed up in Christ.

"He is the light and the life of the world; yea, a light that is endless, that can never be darkened; yea, and also a life which is endless, that there can be no more death."[17]

Jesus Christ Himself declared, "I am the resurrection, and the life: he that believeth in me, though he were dead, yet shall he live."[18]

I testify that through the redeeming Atonement and glorious Resurrection of Jesus Christ, broken hearts can be healed, anguish can become peace, and distress can become hope. He can embrace us in His arms of mercy, comforting, empowering, and healing each of us. In the name of Jesus Christ, amen.

Notes

1. "On a Golden Springtime," *Children's Songbook*, 88.
2. According to the World Health Organization, more than 2.8 million people have died so far from complications related to COVID-19 (see covid19.who.int).
3. Russell M. Nelson, "Doors of Death," *Ensign*, May 1992, 72.
4. See Matthew 27:55; Mark 15:41; Luke 23:49.
5. See Matthew 27:50–55; Mark 15:37–41; Luke 23:44–49; John 19:25–30.
6. Mark 16:10.
7. See Matthew 27:57–60; Mark 15:43–46; Luke 23:50–53; John 19:38.
8. See John 19:39–40.
9. See Matthew 27:61; Mark 15:47; 16:1; Luke 23:55–56; 24:10; John 19:25.
10. See Luke 23:54, 56; John 19:42.
11. See Matthew 28:1–8; Mark 16:2–8; Luke 24:1–12; John 20:1–10.
12. See John 20:11–15.
13. See "Rob Gardner: Portraying the Savior in Music," Apr. 10, 2019, ldsliving.com; Elena Aburto, "Naming Our Grief," Dec. 26, 2019, IWillHealThee.blogspot.com; see also Gospel Topics, "Grief," topics.ChurchofJesusChrist.org; Gospel Topics, "Death, Physical," topics.ChurchofJesusChrist.org; "His Grace," ChurchofJesusChrist.org/media/collection/his-grace.
14. See Mark 16:9–10; John 20:16–18.
15. John 11:23.
16. Russell M. Nelson, "Now Is the Time to Prepare," *Ensign* or *Liahona*, May 2005, 18.
17. Mosiah 16:7–9.
18. John 11:25.

OUR SORROW SHALL BE TURNED INTO JOY

ELDER S. MARK PALMER
Of the Seventy

Several years ago, while attending meetings in Salt Lake City, I was greeted by our dear prophet, Russell M. Nelson. In his typically warm and personal way, he asked, "Mark, how is your mum doing?"

I told him I had been with her earlier that week at her home in New Zealand and that she was getting old but was full of faith and an inspiration to all who knew her.

He then said, "Please give her my love . . . and tell her I look forward to seeing her again."

I was rather surprised and asked, "Do you have a trip planned to New Zealand soon?"

With thoughtful sincerity he replied, "Oh no, I will see her in the next life."

There was nothing frivolous in his response. It was a perfectly natural expression of fact. In that private, unguarded moment, I heard and felt pure testimony from a living prophet that life continues after death.

This conference weekend you will hear living apostles and prophets testify of the Resurrection of Jesus Christ. "The fundamental principles of our religion are the testimony of the Apostles and Prophets, concerning Jesus Christ, that He died, was buried, and rose again the third day[;] . . . all other things which pertain to our religion are only appendages to [this truth]."[1] I promise that as you listen with real intent, the Spirit will confirm in your mind and your heart the truth of these testimonies.[2]

Jesus's ancient Apostles were forever changed after He appeared to them following His death. Ten of them saw for themselves that He had been resurrected. Thomas, being initially absent, declared, "Except I shall see . . . , I will not believe."[3] Later Jesus admonished Thomas, "Be not faithless, but believing."[4] Then the Lord taught the vital role of faith: "Blessed are they that have *not* seen, and yet have believed."[5]

The resurrected Lord gave His Apostles the charge to testify of Him. As with our living Apostles today, they left behind worldly occupations and spent the rest of their lives boldly declaring that God had raised up this Jesus. Their powerful testimonies led to thousands accepting the invitation to be baptized.[6]

The glorious message of Easter morning is central to all Christianity. Jesus Christ has risen from the dead, and because of this, we too will live again after we die. This knowledge gives meaning and purpose to our lives. If we go forward in faith, we will be forever changed, as were the Apostles of old. We, like them, will be able to endure any hardship with faith in Jesus Christ. This faith also gives us hope for a time when our "sorrow shall be turned into joy."[7]

My own faith had its beginnings following a time of sorrow.

My father and mother were sheep farmers in New Zealand.[8] They enjoyed their life. As a young married couple, they were blessed with three little girls. The youngest of these was named Ann. One day while they were on holiday together at a lake, 17-month-old Ann toddled off. After minutes of desperate searching, she was found lifeless in the water.

This nightmare caused unspeakable sorrow. Dad wrote years later that some of the laughter went out of their lives forever. It also caused a yearning for answers to life's most important questions: What will become of our precious Ann? Will we ever see her again? How can our family ever be happy again?

Some years after this tragedy, two young missionaries from The Church of Jesus Christ of Latter-day Saints came to our farm. They began teaching the truths found in the Book of Mormon and the Bible. These truths include the assurance that Ann now lives in the spirit world. Because of the Resurrection of Jesus Christ, she too will be resurrected. They taught that the Church of Jesus Christ has once again been restored on earth with a living prophet and twelve Apostles. And they taught the unique and remarkable doctrine that families can be bound together forever by the same priesthood authority Jesus Christ gave His chief Apostle, Peter.[9]

Mum instantly recognized truth and received a witness of the Spirit. Dad, however, wrestled for the next year between doubts and spiritual nudges. Also, he was reluctant to change his way of life. One morning following a sleepless night, while pacing the floor, he turned to Mum and said, "I will be baptized today or never."

Mum told the missionaries what had happened, and they immediately recognized the flicker of faith in my father that would now be either lit or extinguished.

That very morning our family traveled to the nearest beach. Unaware of what was happening, we children had a picnic on the sand dunes while Elders Boyd Green and Gary Sheffield led my parents into the ocean and baptized them. In a further act of faith, Dad privately committed to the Lord that come what may, he would be true all his life to the promises he was making.

One year later a temple was dedicated in Hamilton, New Zealand. Shortly thereafter our family, with someone representing Ann, knelt around the altar in that sacred house of the Lord. There, by the authority of the priesthood, we were united as an eternal family in a simple and beautiful ordinance. This brought great peace and joy.

Many years later Dad told me that if not for Ann's tragic death, he would never have been humble enough to accept the restored gospel. Yet the Spirit of the Lord instilled hope that what the missionaries taught was true. My parents' faith continued to grow until they each burned with the fire of testimony that quietly and humbly guided their every decision in life.

I will always be thankful for my parents' example to future generations. It is impossible to measure the number of lives forever changed because of their acts of faith in response to profound sorrow.

I invite all who feel sorrow, all who wrestle with doubt, all who wonder what happens after we die, to place your faith in Christ. I promise that if you *desire* to believe, then *act* in faith and *follow* the whisperings of the Spirit, you will find joy in this life and in the world to come.

How I look forward to the day I will meet my sister Ann. I look forward to a joyful reunion with my father, who died over 30 years ago. I testify of the joy to be found in living by faith, *believing without seeing*, but knowing by the power of the Holy Ghost that Jesus Christ lives. With all my heart and soul, I choose to follow Jesus Christ and His restored gospel. This blesses every aspect of my life. I know that Jesus is the Christ, the Son of God, our Savior and our Redeemer. In the name of Jesus Christ, amen.

Notes

1. *Teachings of Presidents of the Church: Joseph Smith* (2007), 49.
2. See Doctrine and Covenants 8:2.
3. John 20:25. "It is common in our secular world to say that 'seeing is believing.' The way of the Lord is best defined by a different maxim: 'Believing is seeing.' Faith in the Lord is the premise, not the conclusion" (Lance B. Wickman, "But If Not," *Ensign* or *Liahona*, Nov. 2002, 31).
4. John 20:27.
5. John 20:29; emphasis added.
6. See Acts 2.
7. John 16:20.
8. Kenneth Molony Palmer and Jill Garlick Palmer.
9. See Matthew 16:19.

PRESSING TOWARD THE MARK

ELDER EDWARD DUBE

Of the Seventy

As I read the book of Acts and Paul's epistles, I am amazed at how Paul was driven by love and gratitude in serving, teaching, and testifying of Jesus Christ. How can such a person serve with such love and gratitude, especially considering his great sufferings? What motivated Paul to serve? "I press toward the mark for the prize of the high calling of God in Christ Jesus."[1]

To press toward the mark is to faithfully continue on the "strait and narrow path which leads to eternal life"[2] with our Savior and our Father in Heaven. Paul viewed his sufferings as "not worthy to be compared with the glory which shall be revealed in us."[3] Paul's letter to the Philippians, which he wrote when he was bound in prison, is a letter of overwhelming joy and rejoicing and encouragement to all of us, particularly in this difficult time of uncertainty. We all need to take courage from Paul: "I count all things but loss for the excellency of the knowledge of Christ Jesus my Lord: for whom I have suffered the loss of all things, and do count them but dung, that I may win Christ."[4]

While we look at Paul's service, we are inspired and uplifted by our own "Pauls" in our day, who also serve, teach, and testify with love and gratitude amidst the challenges they face in their lives and in the lives of their loved ones. An experience I had nine years ago helped me to realize the importance of pressing toward the mark.

In 2012, as I walked for the first time into the general conference leadership meeting, I could not help feeling overwhelmed and inadequate. In my mind there was a voice persistently repeating, "You do not belong here! A serious mistake had been made!" Just as I was walking trying to find a place to sit, Elder Jeffrey R. Holland spotted me. He came to me and said, "Edward, it is good to see you here," and he tenderly patted my face. I felt like a baby! His love and embrace warmed me up and helped me to feel the spirit of belonging, the spirit of brotherhood. On the following day, I observed Elder Holland doing the same thing he had done to me on the previous day, warmly patting then-Elder Dallin H. Oaks's face, who is his senior!

At that moment I felt the Lord's love through these men we sustain as prophets, seers, and revelators. Elder Holland, through his kind, natural actions, helped me to overcome my self-centeredness and my feelings of inadequacy. He helped me to focus on the sacred and joyful work to which I had been called—to bring souls to Christ. He, like Paul of old, pointed me to press toward the mark.

Interestingly, Paul is exhorting us to press forward while calling us to forget that which is behind—our past fears, our past focus, our past failures, and our past sadness. He is inviting us, just like our dear prophet, President Russell M. Nelson, to "a newer, holier approach."[5] The Savior's promise is real: "For whosoever will save his life shall lose it: and whosoever will lose his life for my sake shall find it."[6]

In my first general conference address, I shared an experience of my mother teaching me to work in our field. "Never look back," she said. "Look ahead at what we still have to do."[7]

Toward the end of her life, while Mother battled cancer, she lived with Naume and me. One night I heard her sobbing in her bedroom. Her pain was intense, even after taking her last daily dose of morphine only two hours earlier.

I entered her room and sobbed with her. I prayed aloud for her to receive instant relief from her pain. And then she did the same thing she had done in the field years ago: she stopped and taught me a lesson. I will never forget her face at that moment: frail, stricken, and full of pain, gazing with pity on her sorrowing son. She smiled through her tears, looked directly into my eyes, and said, "It is not up to you or anyone else, but it is up to God whether this pain will go away or not."

I sat up quietly. She too sat quietly. The scene remains vivid in my mind. That night, through my mother, the Lord taught me a lesson that will stay with me forever. As my mother expressed her acceptance of God's will, I remembered the reason Jesus Christ suffered in the Garden of Gethsemane and on the cross at Golgotha. He said: "Behold I have given unto you my gospel, and this is [my] gospel which I have given unto you—that I came into the world to do the will of my Father, because my Father sent me."[8]

I reflect on our dear prophet President Nelson's prophetic questions to us in the last general conference. President Nelson asked: "Are *you* willing to let God prevail in your life? Are *you* willing to let God be the most important influence in your life? . . . Will you allow His voice to take . . . precedence over every other ambition? Are you *willing* to have your will swallowed up in His?"[9] My mother would have responded with an emotional but firm "yes," and other faithful members of the Church across the globe would also respond with an emotional but firm "yes." President Nelson, thank you for inspiring and uplifting us with these prophetic questions.

Recently, I had a conversation in Pretoria, South Africa, with a bishop who buried his wife and his adult daughter on the same day. Their lives were claimed by this coronavirus pandemic. I asked how he was doing. Bishop Teddy Thabethe's response strengthened my resolve to follow the words and counsel from the Lord's prophets, seers, and revelators. Bishop Thabethe responded that there is always hope and comfort in knowing that the Savior has taken upon Himself the pains of His people that He may know how to succor us.[10] With deep faith he testified, "I am grateful for the plan of salvation, the plan of happiness." He then asked me a question: "Is this not what our prophet was trying to teach us this last conference?"

While the challenges of mortality will come to all of us in one way or another, let us focus on the goal of our "press[ing] toward the mark," which is "the prize of the high calling of God."[11]

My humble invitation to all of us is to never give up! We are called to "lay aside every weight, and the sin which doth so easily beset us, and let us run with patience the race that is set before us, looking unto Jesus the author and finisher of our faith."[12]

It is not so much about what we are going through in life but what we are becoming. There is joy in pressing toward the mark. I testify that He who overcame all will help us as we look up to Him. In the name of Jesus Christ, amen.

Notes

1. Philippians 3:14.
2. 2 Nephi 31:18.
3. Romans 8:18; see also 2 Corinthians 1:3–7.
4. Philippians 3:8.
5. Russell M. Nelson, "Ministering," *Ensign* or *Liahona*, May 2018, 100.
6. Matthew 16:25.
7. See Edward Dube, "Look Ahead and Believe," *Ensign* or *Liahona*, Nov. 2013, 15.
8. 3 Nephi 27:13.
9. Russell M. Nelson, "Let God Prevail," *Ensign* or *Liahona*, Nov. 2020, 94.
10. See Alma 7:11–12.
11. Philippians 3:14.
12. Hebrews 12:1–2.

REMEMBER YOUR WAY BACK HOME

ELDER JOSÉ A. TEIXEIRA
Of the Presidency of the Seventy

In 1946, the young researcher Arthur Hasler was hiking along a mountain stream near his boyhood home when he had an experience that led to an important discovery about how fish find their way back to their birth streams.

Hiking up a mountain, yet out of sight of his favorite childhood waterfall, Hasler was suddenly brought back to a forgotten memory. He said, "As a cool breeze, bearing the fragrance of mosses and columbine, swept around the rocky abutment, the details of this waterfall and its setting on the face of the mountain suddenly leapt into my mind's eye."[1]

These smells rekindled his childhood memories and reminded him of home.

If smells could trigger such memories for him, he reasoned that perhaps smells could be as evocative for salmon who, after years of being in the open ocean, return to the exact stream of their birth to spawn.

Based on this experience, Hasler, together with other researchers, went on to demonstrate that salmon remember the very scents that would help them navigate thousands of miles to find their way back home from the sea.

This account caused me to think that one of the most important things we can do in this life is to recognize and remember the pathway back to our Heavenly Father and faithfully and joyfully persevere throughout the journey.

I thought of four reminders that, when used and applied consistently in our lives, can rekindle feelings of our heavenly home.

First, We Can Remember That We Are Children of God

We have a divine heritage. Knowing that we are children of God and that He wants us to return to His presence is one of the first steps on the journey back to our heavenly home.

Remind yourself of this heritage. Make time regularly to boost your spiritual immune system by remembering the blessings you have received from the Lord. Trust the guides you have been given from Him, rather than turning solely to the world to measure your personal worth and find your way.

Recently I visited a loved one after she had been in the hospital. She told me with emotion that while she was lying in the hospital bed, all she desired was for someone to sing to her the song "I Am a Child of God." That thought alone, she said, gave her the peace she needed in that hour of affliction.

Knowing who you are changes what you feel and what you do.

Understanding who you truly are better prepares you to recognize and remember your way back to your heavenly home and yearn to be there.

Second, We Can Remember the Foundation That Protects Us

Strength comes to us when we remain righteous, true, and faithful to Heavenly Father and Jesus Christ, even when others overwhelmingly disregard the commandments and principles of salvation.[2]

In the Book of Mormon, Helaman taught his sons to remember that they must build their foundations on Jesus Christ in order to have the strength to withstand the temptations of the adversary. Satan's mighty winds and storms are beating upon us, but they will have no power to drag us down if we put our trust in the safest place—in our Redeemer.[3]

I know from personal experience that as we choose to hear His voice and follow Him, we will receive His help. We will obtain a wider perspective of our circumstances and a deeper understanding of the purpose of life. We will feel the spiritual stirrings that will guide us to our heavenly home.

Third, We Can Remember to Be Prayerful

We live in a time when with a single touch or voice command, we can begin searching for answers on almost any topic in the immensity of data stored and organized in a vast and complex network of computers.

On the other hand, we have the simplicity of the invitation to begin seeking answers from heaven. "Pray always, and I will pour out my Spirit upon you." Then the Lord promises, "And great shall be your blessing—yea, even more than if you should obtain treasures of earth."[4]

God is fully aware of each one of us and ready to listen to our prayers. When we remember to pray, we find His sustaining love, and the more we pray to our Father in Heaven in Christ's name, the more we bring the Savior into our life and the better we will recognize the path He has marked to our heavenly home.

Fourth, We Can Remember to Serve Others

As we strive to follow Jesus Christ by serving and showing kindness to others, we make the world a better place.

Our actions can significantly bless the lives of those around us and our own lives as well. Loving service adds meaning to the lives of both the giver and the receiver.

Do not underestimate the potential you have to influence others for good, both by the service of your actions and by the service of your example.

Loving service to others guides us along the path to our heavenly home—the path of becoming like our Savior.

In 1975, as a result of a civil war, Arnaldo and Eugenia Teles Grilo and their children had to leave behind their home and all that they had built through decades of hard work. Back in their native country of Portugal, Brother and Sister Teles Grilo faced the challenge of starting all over again. But years later, after joining The Church of Jesus Christ of Latter-day Saints, they said, "We lost everything we had, but it was a good thing because it compelled us to consider the importance of eternal blessings."[5]

They lost their earthly home, but they found the way back to their heavenly home.

Whatever you must leave behind to follow the path to your heavenly home will one day seem like no sacrifice at all.

We have Jesus Christ's perfect example to follow, and the journey toward our eternal home is possible only because of His teachings, His life, and His atoning sacrifice—including His death and glorious Resurrection.

I invite you to experience the joy of remembering that we are children of God and that He so loved the world that He has sent His Son[6] to show us the path. I invite you to remember to be faithful, to turn your life to the Savior and build your foundation on Him. Remember to be prayerful in your journey and serve others along the way.

Dear brothers and sisters, on this Easter Sunday, I bear testimony that Jesus Christ is the Redeemer and Savior of the world. He is the one who can usher us to the table of a joyful life and guide us in our journey. May we remember and follow Him home. In the name of Jesus Christ, amen.

Notes

1. Arthur Davis Hasler, in Gene E. Likens, "Arthur Davis Hasler: January 5, 1908–March 23, 2001," in National Academy of Sciences, *Biographical Memoirs*, vol. 82 (2003), 174–75.
2. See *Book of Mormon Student Manual* (2009), 268–73.
3. See Helaman 5:6–12.
4. Doctrine and Covenants 19:38.
5. See Don L. Searle, "Discovering Gospel Riches in Portugal," *Ensign*, Oct. 1987, 15.
6. See John 3:16.

GOD LOVES HIS CHILDREN

ELDER TANIELA B. WAKOLO
Of the Seventy

Brothers and sisters, I rejoice with you in the gospel of Jesus Christ. I bring with me love from the resilient members in the Philippines and say, on their behalf, *Mabuhay*!

On this Easter morning, I testify of the living Christ, that He rose from the dead and that His love for us and for our Father in Heaven is pure and eternal. Today, I desire to focus on the love of Heavenly Father and Jesus Christ for all, which is manifest through the Atonement of Jesus Christ. "For God so loved the world, that he gave his only begotten Son" (John 3:16).

When the prophet Nephi was asked by an angel about his knowledge of God, Nephi responded simply, "I know that he loveth his children" (see 1 Nephi 11:16–17).

A verse from the Book of Mormon: Another Testament of Jesus Christ powerfully describes the Savior's perfect love: "And the world, because of their iniquity, shall judge him to be a thing of naught; . . . they scourge him, . . . they smite him, . . . they spit upon him, and he suffereth it, because of his loving kindness and his long-suffering towards the children of men" (1 Nephi 19:9). The Savior's universal love is the motivating force behind all that He does. We know that it is the same love our Father in Heaven has for us, because the Savior humbly taught that He and the Father "are one" (see John 10:30; 17:20–23).

How, then, do we reciprocate and show our gratitude for Their universal love? The Savior taught us with this simple, all-encompassing invitation: "If ye love me, keep my commandments" (John 14:15).

President Dallin H. Oaks taught, "God's universal and perfect love is shown in all the blessings of His gospel plan, including the fact that His choicest blessings are reserved for those who obey His laws."[1]

I would like to share three specific ways our Heavenly Father manifests His love for us, His children.

First, Relationships with God and Family Manifest His Love

Our most valuable relationships are with the Father and the Son and with our own families because our ties to them are eternal. The great plan of happiness is a wonderful manifestation of God's love for us. With eyes riveted on God's plan, we willingly choose to carve out soil and rocks within us that support selfish desires and replace them with foundations that build eternal relationships. In a sense, this can be called "spiritual excavation." In performing our spiritual excavation, we must first seek after God and call upon Him (see Jeremiah 29:12–13).

Seeking after Him and calling upon Him will begin the process and provide space to build and strengthen our eternal relationships. It broadens our spiritual view and helps us focus on changing what we can control rather than on fears outside our control. Studying the life and ministry of our Savior, Jesus Christ, will enable us to view these other concerns with an eternal perspective.

Distractions can sometimes prevent us from experiencing God's love in our family relationships and activities. A mother, feeling that gadgets were taking over her family relationships, came up with a solution. At the dinner table and at other family times, she just calls out, "Phones on the deck; let us have face time." She says that this is the new norm for their family and that it strengthens their relationship as a family when they have real face time. They now enjoy quality *Come, Follow Me* discussions together as a family.

Second, He Manifests His Love to His Children by Calling Prophets

Our current world is deluged in a "war of words and tumult of opinions" (Joseph Smith—History 1:10). Paul reminds us that "there are . . . so many kinds of voices in the world" (1 Corinthians 14:10). Which of all the voices rise clearly and meaningfully above the fray? It is the voice of God's prophets, seers, and revelators.

I remember vividly, after undergoing surgery in 2018 and upon returning to work, I was in the parking garage at Church headquarters. Suddenly, I heard the voice of President Russell M. Nelson calling, "Taniela, Taniela." I ran toward him, and he asked how I was doing.

I said, "I am recovering very well, President Nelson."

He gave me counsel and a hug. I truly felt the personal ministry of a prophet to the "one."

President Nelson has traveled to many nations of the earth. In my mind, he is not just ministering to thousands, but he is ministering to thousands of "ones." In doing so, he shares the love God has for all His children.

Recently, the words of President Nelson have been a source of strength and inspiration to the people of the Philippines. As with every country in the world, during 2020 the Philippines was severely affected by the COVID-19 pandemic, as well as a volcanic eruption, earthquakes, strong typhoons, and devastating floods.

But like a pillar of light shining through dark clouds of fear, loneliness, and despair came the words of the prophet. They included the call for worldwide fasting and prayer and counsel to move forward despite the pandemic. He invited us to make our homes personal sanctuaries of faith. He called upon Latter-day Saints everywhere to respect all of God's children and to let God prevail in our lives.[2]

Likewise stirring were President Nelson's recent video testimony about the power of gratitude and his concluding prayer, which resonated across the Philippines.[3] In the province of Leyte, the video was played during an interfaith event, and it was also mentioned as part of a priest's homily. The Philippines, along with the entire world, are so blessed to feel God's love through the words of His chosen prophet.

Third, Chastening Can Be a Manifestation of God's Love for His Children

Sometimes God manifests His love by chastening us. It is a way of reminding us that He loves us and that He knows who we are.

His promised blessing of peace is open to all those who courageously walk the covenant path and are willing to receive correction.

When we recognize the chastening and are willing recipients, it becomes a spiritual surgery. Who likes surgery, by the way? But to those who need it and are willing to receive it, it can be lifesaving. The Lord chastens whom He loves. The scriptures tell us so (see Hebrews 12:5–11; Helaman 12:3; Doctrine and Covenants 1:27; 95:1). That chastening, or spiritual surgery, will bring about needed change in our lives. We will realize, brothers and sisters, that it refines and purifies our inner vessels.

Joseph Smith, the Prophet of the Restoration, was chastened. After Joseph lost the 116 pages of the Book of Mormon manuscript, the Lord both corrected and showed love by saying: "You should not have feared man more than God. . . . You should have been faithful. . . . Behold, thou art Joseph, and thou wast chosen. . . . Remember, God is merciful; therefore, repent" (Doctrine and Covenants 3:7–10).

In 2016, while serving a mission in Little Rock, Arkansas, I asked Brother Cava to deliver a package to my older sister, who lived on an island in Fiji. His response was not something that I had anticipated. "President Wakolo," he groaned, "your sister passed away and was buried 10 days ago." I had self-pity and even felt a little upset that my family did not even bother to let me know.

The next day, while my wife was teaching missionaries, this thought penetrated my soul: "Taniela, all these experiences are for your own good and development. You have been teaching and sharing your testimony about the Atonement of Jesus Christ; now live accordingly." I was reminded that "happy is the man whom God correct[s]: therefore [we should] despise not . . . the chastening of the Almighty" (Job 5:17). It was a spiritual surgery for me, and the outcome was immediate.

Just as I was contemplating the experience, I was called upon to give my concluding thoughts to the discussion. Among other things, I shared the lessons that I had just been taught: one, I had just been chastened by the Holy Ghost, and I loved it because I was the only one who heard it; two, because of the Savior's sacrifice and ransom, I will no longer refer to my challenges as trials and tribulations but as my learning experiences; and three, because of His perfect and sinless life, I will no longer refer to my shortcomings and lack of abilities as weaknesses but rather as my development opportunities. This experience helped me know that God chastens us because He loves us.

I conclude. Our Eternal Father and His Son, Jesus Christ, show Their love by making it possible for us to have eternal relationships with Them and our family members, by calling modern-day prophets to teach and minister to us, and by chastening us to help us learn and grow. "God be thanked for the matchless gift of His divine Son,"[4] our resurrected Lord, even the living Christ. In the name of Jesus Christ, amen.

Notes

1. Dallin H. Oaks, "Love and Law," *Ensign* or *Liahona*, Nov. 2009, 26.
2. See Russell M. Nelson, "Opening the Heavens for Help," *Ensign* or *Liahona*, May 2020, 73–74; "Embrace the Future with Faith," *Ensign* or *Liahona*, Nov. 2020, 73–76; "Let God Prevail," *Ensign* or *Liahona*, Nov. 2020, 92–95.
3. See "President Russell M. Nelson on the Healing Power of Gratitude" (video), ChurchofJesusChrist.org.
4. "The Living Christ: The Testimony of the Apostles," ChurchofJesusChrist.org.

THEY CANNOT PREVAIL; WE CANNOT FALL

ELDER CHI HONG (SAM) WONG
Of the Seventy

Our dear prophet, President Russell M. Nelson, said in our last general conference: "During these perilous times of which the Apostle Paul prophesied, Satan is no longer even *trying* to hide his attacks on God's plan. Emboldened evil abounds. Therefore, the only way to survive spiritually is to be determined to let God prevail in our lives, to learn to hear His voice, and to use our energy to help gather Israel."[1]

As we consider the prophet's invitation to learn to hear God's voice, are our hearts determined or hardened? Let us remember the counsel given in Jacob 6:6: "Yea, today, if ye will hear his voice, harden not your hearts; for why will ye die?" Let us be determined to let God prevail in our lives.

How can we let God prevail in our lives and not the adversary? In Doctrine and Covenants 6:34 we read, "Therefore, fear not, little flock; do good; let earth and hell combine against you, for if ye are built upon my rock, they cannot prevail." It is a significant promise. Although earth and hell may combine against us, they cannot prevail if we choose to let God prevail by establishing our lives upon His rock.

Speaking to His disciples, Jesus Christ taught of a wise man and a foolish man, recorded in Matthew chapter 7 of the New Testament. Many of you have heard the Primary song "The Wise Man and the Foolish Man."[2] If you have taken the time to compare the four verses in the song, you will find that verses 1 and 2 are very similar to verses 3 and 4. Both the wise man and the foolish man were building a house. They want to provide their family with a safe and comfortable home. They desire to live happily together forever as a family, just like you and me. The surrounding situation was the same: "The *rains* came down, and the *floods* came up." We sing it six times when we sing that song. The only difference is that the wise man built his house upon the rock and the house stood still, whereas the foolish man built his house upon the sand and his house washed away. Therefore, where our foundation is really matters, and this has a decisive effect on the outcome ultimately and eternally.

I hope and pray that we all will find and stay on the sure foundation as we establish our future life. We are reminded in Helaman 5:12: "And now, my sons, remember, remember that it is upon the rock of our Redeemer, who is Christ, the Son of God, that ye must build your foundation; that when the devil shall send forth his mighty winds, yea, his shafts in the whirlwind, yea, when all his hail and his mighty storm shall beat upon you, it shall have no power over you to drag you down to the gulf of misery and endless wo, because of the rock upon which ye are built, which is a sure foundation, a foundation whereon if men build they cannot fall."

That is the promise from God! If we build our foundation on Jesus Christ, we cannot fall! As we endure faithfully to the end, God will help us establish our lives upon His rock, "and the gates of hell shall not prevail against [us]" (Doctrine and Covenants 10:69). We may not be able to change all of what is coming, but we can choose how we prepare for what is coming.

Some of us may think, "The gospel is good, so we need to put it in our lives, maybe once a week." Just going to church once a week is not enough to build upon the rock. Our entire lives should be filled with the gospel of Jesus Christ. The gospel is not part of our life, but our life is actually part of the gospel of Jesus Christ. Think about it. Is that not true? Our mortal life is only part of the whole plan of salvation and exaltation.

God is our Heavenly Father. He loves all of us. He knows our potential way better than we know ourselves. He knows not only the details of our lives. God knows the details of the details of the details of our lives.

Please follow our living prophet President Nelson's wise counsel. As recorded in Doctrine and Covenants 21:5–6:

"For his word ye shall receive, as if from mine own mouth, in all patience and faith.

"For by doing these things the gates of hell shall not prevail against you; yea, and the Lord God will disperse the powers of darkness from before you, and cause the heavens to shake for your good, and his name's glory."

For that reason, they cannot prevail, and we cannot fall!

I testify to you that Christ will come again a second time as He did the first time, but this time it will be with great glory and majesty. I hope and pray that I will be ready to receive Him, whether on this side of the veil or on the other side. As we celebrate in this wonderful Easter season, I hope, through the Atonement of Jesus Christ and the power of His Resurrection (see Moroni 7:41), I will be able to go up and meet with my Maker and say, "Thank you." In the name of Jesus Christ, amen.

Notes

1. Russell M. Nelson, "Let God Prevail," *Ensign* or *Liahona*, Nov. 2020, 95.
2. "The Wise Man and the Foolish Man," *Children's Songbook*, 281.

OUR PERSONAL SAVIOR

ELDER MICHAEL JOHN U. TEH

Of the Seventy

I am grateful to be with you this wonderful Easter morning. When I think of Easter, I love to rehearse in my mind the words spoken by angels to those who were at the Garden Tomb: "Why seek ye the living among the dead? He is not here, but is risen."[1] I testify that Jesus of Nazareth was resurrected and He lives.

What Think Ye of Christ?

Thirty-four years ago, my missionary companion and I met and taught a very intellectual man who was a contributing writer for a local newspaper in Davao City, Philippines. We enjoyed teaching him because he had a lot of questions and was very respectful of our beliefs. The most memorable question he asked us was "What think ye of Christ?"[2] We of course excitedly shared our feelings and bore testimony of Jesus Christ. He later published an article on the same topic that contained wonderful words and phrases about the Savior. I remember being impressed but not necessarily lifted. It had good information but felt hollow and lacked spiritual power.

Increasingly Coming to Know Him

"What think ye of Christ?" I am realizing that how intimately I know the Savior significantly influences my ability to hear Him as well as how I respond. A few years ago, Elder David A. Bednar asked the following questions as part of his remarks: "Do we only know about the Savior, or are we increasingly coming to know Him? How do we come to know the Lord?"[3]

As I studied and pondered, I came to the stark realization that what I know about the Savior greatly outweighed how much I really know Him. I resolved then to put forth more effort to know Him. I am very grateful for the scriptures and testimonies of faithful men and women disciples of Jesus Christ. My own journey over the last few years has taken me down many roads of study and discovery.

I pray that the Holy Ghost will convey to you today a message far greater than the inadequate words that I have written.

First, we need to recognize that knowing the Savior is the most important pursuit of our lives. It should take priority over anything else.

"And this is life eternal, that they might know thee the only true God, and Jesus Christ, whom thou hast sent."[4]

"Jesus saith unto him, I am the way, the truth, and the life: no man cometh unto the Father, but by me."[5]

"I am the light of the world: he that followeth me shall not walk in darkness, but shall have the light of life."[6]

Second, as we are increasingly coming to know the Savior, scriptural passages and the words of the prophets become so intimately meaningful to us that they become our own words. It is not about copying the words, feelings, and experiences of others as much as it is coming to know for ourselves, in our own unique way, by experimenting upon the word[7] and receiving a witness from the Holy Ghost. As the prophet Alma declared:

"Do ye not suppose that I know of these things myself? Behold, I testify unto you that I do know that these things whereof I have spoken are true. And how do ye suppose that I know of their surety?

"Behold, I say unto you they are made known unto me by the Holy Spirit of God. Behold, I have fasted and prayed many days that I might know these things of myself. And now I do know of myself that they are true; for the Lord God hath made them manifest unto me by his Holy Spirit; and this is the spirit of revelation which is in me."[8]

Third, an increasing understanding that the Atonement of Jesus Christ applies to us personally and individually will help us know Him. Oftentimes it is easier for us to think and speak of Christ's Atonement in general terms than to recognize its personal significance in our lives. The Atonement of Jesus Christ is infinite and eternal and all-encompassing in its breadth and depth but wholly personal and individual in its effects. Because of His atoning sacrifice, the Savior has power to cleanse, heal, and strengthen us one by one.

The Savior's only desire, His only purpose from the very beginning, was to do the will of the Father. The will of the Father was for Him to assist in "[bringing] to pass the immortality and eternal life of man"[9] by becoming our "advocate with the Father."[10] Hence, "though he were a Son, yet learned he obedience by the things which he suffered; and being made perfect, he became the author of eternal salvation unto all them that obey him."[11]

"And he shall go forth, suffering pains and afflictions and temptations of every kind. . . .

"And he will take upon him death, that he may loose the bands of death . . . and he will take upon him their infirmities, that his bowels may be filled with mercy, . . . that he may know according to the flesh how to succor his people according to their infirmities.

". . . The Son of God suffereth according to the flesh that he might take upon him the sins of his people, that he might blot out their transgressions according to the power of his deliverance."[12]

I would like to share a simple experience that illustrates the struggle we sometimes have to embrace the personal nature of the Lord's Atonement.

Years ago, at the invitation of my file leader, I read the Book of Mormon from cover to cover and marked the verses that referenced the Lord's Atonement. My leader also invited me to prepare a one-page summary of what I learned. I said to myself, "One page? Sure, that is easy." To my surprise, however, I found the task to be extremely difficult, and I failed.

I have since realized that I failed because I missed the mark and had incorrect assumptions. First, I expected the summary to be inspiring to everyone. The summary was meant for me and not for anyone else. It was meant to capture my feelings and emotions about the Savior and what He has done for me so that every time I read it, it will bring to the surface wonderful, poignant, and personal spiritual experiences.

Second, I expected the summary to be grand and elaborate and contain big words and phrases. It was never about big words. It was meant to be a clear and simple declaration of conviction. "For my soul delighteth in plainness; for after this manner doth the Lord God work among the children of men. For the Lord God giveth light unto the understanding."[13]

Third, I expected it to be perfect, a summary to end all summaries—a final summary that one cannot and should not add to—instead of a work in progress to which I can add a word here or a phrase there as my understanding of Jesus Christ's Atonement increases.

Testimony and Invitation

As a young man, I learned a lot from my conversations with my bishop. During those tender years, I learned to love these words from a favorite hymn:

> *I stand all amazed at the love Jesus offers me,*
> *Confused at the grace that so fully he proffers me.*
> *I tremble to know that for me he was crucified,*
> *That for me, a sinner, he suffered, he bled and died.*
> *Oh, it is wonderful that he should care for me*
> *Enough to die for me!*
> *Oh, it is wonderful, wonderful to me!*[14]

The prophet Moroni invited us: "And now, I would commend you to seek this Jesus of whom the prophets and apostles have written."[15]

President Russell M. Nelson promised that "if [we] proceed to learn *all* [we] can about Jesus Christ, . . . [our] ability to turn away from sin will increase. [Our] desire to keep the commandments will soar."[16]

On this Easter Sunday, just as the Savior came forth from His stone grave, may we awake from our spiritual slumber and rise above the clouds of doubt, the clutches of fear, the intoxication of pride, and the lull of complacency. Jesus Christ and Heavenly Father live. I testify of Their perfect love for us. In the name of Jesus Christ, amen.

Notes

1. Luke 24:5–6.
2. Matthew 22:42.
3. David A. Bednar, "If Ye Had Known Me," *Ensign* or *Liahona*, Nov. 2016, 103.
4. John 17:3.
5. John 14:6.
6. John 8:12.
7. See Alma 32:27.
8. Alma 5:45–46.
9. Moses 1:39.
10. 1 John 2:1.
11. Hebrews 5:8–9.
12. Alma 7:11–13.
13. 2 Nephi 31:3.
14. "I Stand All Amazed," *Hymns*, no. 193.
15. Ether 12:41.
16. Russell M. Nelson, "Prophets, Leadership, and Divine Law" (worldwide devotional for young adults, Jan. 8, 2017), broadcasts.ChurchofJesusChrist.org.

CHRIST IS RISEN; FAITH IN HIM WILL MOVE MOUNTAINS

PRESIDENT RUSSELL M. NELSON

President of The Church of Jesus Christ of Latter-day Saints

My dear brothers and sisters, I am grateful for the privilege of speaking with you on this Easter Sunday.[1] The atoning sacrifice and Resurrection of Jesus Christ changed each of our lives forever. We love Him and gratefully worship Him and our Heavenly Father.

During the past six months, we have continued to grapple with a global pandemic. I marvel at your resilience and spiritual strength in the face of illness, loss, and isolation. I pray constantly that, through it all, you will feel the Lord's unfailing love for you. If you have responded to your trials with a stronger discipleship, this past year will not have been in vain.

This morning, we have heard from Church leaders who come from every populated continent on earth. Truly, the blessings of the gospel are for *every* race, language, and people. The Church of Jesus Christ is a *global* church. Jesus Christ is our leader.

Thankfully, even a pandemic has not been able to slow the onward march of His truth. The gospel of Jesus Christ is exactly what is needed in this confused, contentious, and weary world.

Each of God's children deserves the opportunity to hear and accept the healing, redeeming message of Jesus Christ. No other message is more vital to our happiness—now and forever.[2] No other message is more filled with hope. No other message can eliminate contention in our society.

Faith in Jesus Christ is the foundation of all belief and the conduit of divine power. According to the Apostle Paul, "Without faith it is impossible to please [God]: for he that cometh to God must believe that he is, and that he is a rewarder of them that diligently seek him."[3]

Everything good in life—every potential blessing of eternal significance—begins with faith. Allowing God to prevail in our lives begins with faith that He is willing to guide us. True repentance begins with faith that Jesus Christ has the power to cleanse, heal, and strengthen us.[4]

"Deny not the power of God," the prophet Moroni declared, "for he worketh by power, *according to the faith* of the children of men."[5] It is *our* faith that unlocks the power of God in *our* lives.

And yet, exercising faith can seem overwhelming. At times we may wonder if we can possibly muster enough faith to receive the blessings that we so desperately need. However, the Lord put those fears to rest through the words of the Book of Mormon prophet Alma.

Alma asks us simply to *experiment* upon the word and "exercise a *particle* of faith, yea, even if [we] can no more than desire to believe."[6] The phrase "particle of faith" reminds me of the Lord's biblical promise that if we "have faith as a *grain of mustard seed*," we shall be able to "say unto this mountain, Remove hence to yonder place; and it shall remove; and *nothing shall be impossible unto [us]*."[7]

The Lord understands our mortal weakness. We all falter at times. But He also knows of our great potential. The mustard seed starts small but grows into a tree large enough for birds to nest in its branches. The mustard seed represents a small but *growing* faith.[8]

The Lord does not require *perfect* faith for us to have access to His *perfect* power. But He does ask us to believe.

My dear brothers and sisters, my call to you this Easter morning is to *start today* to increase your faith. Through your faith, Jesus Christ will increase your ability to move the mountains in your life,[9] even though your personal challenges may loom as large as Mount Everest.

Your mountains may be loneliness, doubt, illness, or other personal problems. Your mountains will vary, and yet the answer to each of your challenges is to increase your faith. That takes work. Lazy learners and lax disciples will always struggle to muster even a particle of faith.

To do anything well requires effort. Becoming a true disciple of Jesus Christ is no exception. Increasing your faith and trust in Him takes effort. May I offer five suggestions to help you develop that faith and trust.

First, **study**. Become an engaged learner. Immerse yourself in the scriptures to understand better Christ's mission and ministry. Know the doctrine of Christ so that you understand its power for your life. Internalize the truth that the Atonement of Jesus Christ applies to *you*. He took upon Himself *your* misery, *your* mistakes, *your* weakness, and *your* sins. He paid the compensatory price and provided the power for you to move *every* mountain you will ever face. You obtain that power with your faith, trust, and willingness to follow Him.

Moving your mountains may require a miracle. Learn about miracles. Miracles come according to your faith in the Lord. Central to that faith is trusting His will and timetable—how and when He will bless you with the miraculous help you desire. Only *your* unbelief will keep God from blessing you with miracles to move the mountains in *your* life.[10]

The more you learn about the Savior, the easier it will be to trust in His mercy, His infinite love, and His strengthening, healing, and redeeming power. The Savior is never closer to you than when you are facing or climbing a mountain *with faith*.

Second, choose to **believe** in Jesus Christ. If you have doubts about God the Father and His Beloved Son or the validity of the Restoration or the veracity of Joseph Smith's divine calling as a prophet, *choose* to believe[11] and stay faithful. Take your questions to the Lord and to other faithful sources. Study with the desire to *believe* rather than with the hope that you can find a flaw in the fabric of a prophet's life or a discrepancy in the scriptures. Stop increasing your doubts by rehearsing them with other doubters. Allow the Lord to lead you on your journey of spiritual discovery.

Third, **act** in faith. What would you do if you had *more* faith? Think about it. Write about it. Then *receive more* faith by doing something that *requires more* faith.

Fourth, **partake of sacred ordinances** worthily. Ordinances unlock the power of God for your life.[12]

And fifth, **ask** your Heavenly Father, in the name of Jesus Christ, for help.

Faith takes work. Receiving revelation takes work. But "every one that asketh receiveth; and he that seeketh findeth; and to him that knocketh it shall be opened."[13] God knows what will help your faith grow. Ask, and then ask again.

A nonbeliever might say that faith is for the weak. But this assertion overlooks the *power* of faith. Would the Savior's Apostles have continued to teach His doctrine after His death, at the peril of their lives, if they had doubted Him?[14] Would Joseph and Hyrum Smith have suffered martyrs' deaths defending the Restoration of the Lord's Church unless they had a sure witness that it was true? Would nearly 2,000 Saints have died along the pioneer trail[15] if they did not have faith that the gospel of Jesus Christ had been restored? Truly, faith is the power that *enables* the unlikely to accomplish the impossible.

Do not minimize the faith you already have. It takes faith to join the Church and remain faithful. It takes faith to follow prophets rather than pundits and popular opinion. It takes faith to serve a mission during a pandemic. It takes faith to live a chaste life when the world shouts that God's law of chastity is now outmoded. It takes faith to teach the gospel to children in a secular world. It takes faith to plead for the life of a loved one and even more faith to accept a disappointing answer.

Two years ago, Sister Nelson and I visited Samoa, Tonga, Fiji, and Tahiti. Each of those island nations had experienced heavy rains for days. Members had fasted and prayed that their outdoor meetings would be protected from the rain.

In Samoa, Fiji, and Tahiti, *just* as the meetings began, the rain stopped. But in Tonga, the rain did *not* stop. Yet 13,000 faithful Saints came hours early to get a seat, waited patiently through a steady downpour, and then sat through a very wet two-hour meeting.

We saw vibrant faith at work among each of those islanders—faith sufficient to stop the rain and faith to persevere when the rain did not stop.

The mountains in our lives do not always move how or when we would like. But our faith will *always* propel us forward. Faith *always* increases our access to godly power.

Please know this: if everything and everyone else in the world whom you trust should fail, Jesus Christ and His Church will *never* fail you. The Lord never slumbers, nor does He sleep.[16] He "is the same yesterday, today, and [tomorrow]."[17] He will not forsake His covenants,[18] His promises, or His love for His people. He works miracles today, and He will work miracles tomorrow.[19]

Faith in Jesus Christ is the *greatest power* available to us in this life. All things are possible to them that believe.[20]

Your *growing* faith in Him will move mountains—not the mountains of rock that beautify the earth but the mountains of misery in your lives. Your *flourishing* faith will help you turn challenges into unparalleled growth and opportunity.

On this Easter Sunday, with my deep feelings of love and gratitude, I declare my witness that Jesus Christ is indeed risen. He is risen to lead His Church. He is risen to bless the lives of all of God's children, wherever they live. With faith in Him, we can move the mountains in our lives. I so testify in the sacred name of Jesus Christ, amen.

Notes

1. In some parts of the world, people use a unique and special way of exchanging greetings on Easter morning. In their local language, the greeter will say, "Christ is risen!" The greeted person then responds, "Truly! He is risen!" For example, the exchange of Easter greetings by Russian speakers begins with "Христос воскрес" (Christ is risen [resurrected]!), answered by "Воистину! воскрес!" (Truly! He is risen!).
2. See Mosiah 2:41.
3. Hebrews 11:6. *Lectures on Faith* states that faith "is the first great governing principle which has power, dominion, and authority over all things" ([1985], 5).
4. See Matthew 11:28–30; Alma 7:12–13; Ether 12:27.
5. Moroni 10:7; emphasis added.
6. Alma 32:27; emphasis added.
7. Matthew 17:20, emphasis added; see also Helaman 12:9, 13.
8. See Doctrine and Covenants 78:17–18. The reward for putting off the natural man is to become "a saint through the atonement of Christ the Lord" (Mosiah 3:19).
9. See 1 Nephi 7:12.
10. See Mormon 9:19–21; Ether 12:30.
11. See 2 Nephi 33:10–11.
12. See Doctrine and Covenants 84:20.
13. Matthew 7:8.
14. Without the power of faith, would Abinadi have suffered death by fire for refusing to deny what

he knew to be true? (see Mosiah 17:7–20). Without that power, would Ether have hidden in the cavity of a rock (see Ether 13:13–14) and Moroni endured years of loneliness (see Moroni 1:1–3) when their lives could have been much more comfortable if they had only denounced what they believed?

15. See Melvin L. Bashore, H. Dennis Tolley, and the BYU Pioneer Mortality Team, "Mortality on the Mormon Trail, 1847–1868," *BYU Studies*, vol. 53, no. 4 (2014), 115.
16. See Psalm 121:4.
17. Mormon 9:9.
18. See Isaiah 54:10; 3 Nephi 22:10.
19. See Mormon 9:10–11, 15.
20. See Mark 9:23.

SUNDAY AFTERNOON SESSION

APRIL 4, 2021

DEFENDING OUR DIVINELY INSPIRED CONSTITUTION

PRESIDENT DALLIN H. OAKS

First Counselor in the First Presidency

In this troubled time, I have felt to speak about the inspired Constitution of the United States. This Constitution is of special importance to our members in the United States, but it is also a common heritage of constitutions around the world.

I.

A constitution is the foundation of government. It provides structure and limits for the exercise of government powers. The United States Constitution is the oldest written constitution still in force today. Though originally adopted by only a small number of colonies, it soon became a model worldwide. Today, every nation except three have adopted written constitutions.[1]

In these remarks I do not speak for any political party or other group. I speak for the United States Constitution, which I have studied for more than 60 years. I speak from my experience as a law clerk to the chief justice of the United States Supreme Court. I speak from my 15 years as a professor of law and my 3½ years as a justice on the Utah Supreme Court. Most important, I speak from 37 years as an Apostle of Jesus Christ, responsible to study the meaning of the divinely inspired United States Constitution to the work of His restored Church.

The United States Constitution is unique because God revealed that He "established" it "for the rights and protection of all flesh" (Doctrine and Covenants 101:77; see also verse 80). That is why this constitution is of special concern for The Church of Jesus Christ of Latter-day Saints throughout the world. Whether or how its principles should be applied in other nations of the world is for them to decide.

What was God's purpose in establishing the United States Constitution? We see it in the doctrine of moral agency. In the first decade of the restored Church, its members on the western frontier were suffering private and public persecution. Partly this was because of their opposition to the human slavery then existing in the United States. In these unfortunate circumstances, God revealed through the Prophet Joseph Smith eternal truths about His doctrine.

God has given His children moral agency—the power to decide and to act. The most desirable condition for the exercise of that agency is maximum freedom for men and women to act according to their individual choices. Then, the revelation explains, "every man may be accountable for his own sins in the day of judgment" (Doctrine and Covenants 101:78). "Therefore," the Lord revealed, "it is not right that any man should be in bondage one to another" (Doctrine and Covenants 101:79). This obviously means that human slavery is wrong. And according to the same principle, it is wrong for citizens to have no voice in the selection of their rulers or the making of their laws.

II.

Our belief that the United States Constitution was divinely inspired does not mean that divine revelation dictated every word and phrase, such as the provisions allocating the number of representatives from each state or the minimum age of each.[2] The Constitution was not "a fully grown document," said President J. Reuben Clark. "On the contrary," he explained, "we believe it must grow and develop to meet the changing needs of an advancing world."[3] For example, inspired *amendments* abolished slavery and gave women the right to vote. However, we do not see inspiration in every Supreme Court decision interpreting the Constitution.

I believe the United States Constitution contains at least five divinely inspired principles.[4]

First is the principle that the source of government power is the people. In a time when sovereign power was universally assumed to come from the divine right of kings or from military power, attributing sovereign power to the people was revolutionary. Philosophers had advocated this, but the United States Constitution was the first to apply it. Sovereign power in the people does *not* mean that mobs or other groups of people can intervene to intimidate or force government action. The Constitution established a constitutional democratic republic, where the people exercise their power through their elected representatives.

A second inspired principle is the division of delegated power between the nation and its subsidiary states. In our federal system, this unprecedented principle has sometimes been altered by inspired amendments, such as those abolishing slavery and extending voting rights to women, mentioned earlier. Significantly, the United States Constitution limits the national government to the exercise of powers granted expressly or by implication, and it reserves all other government powers "to the States respectively, or to the people."[5]

Another inspired principle is the separation of powers. Well over a century before our 1787 Constitutional Convention, the English Parliament pioneered the separation of legislative and executive authority when they wrested certain powers from the king. The inspiration in the American convention was to delegate *independent* executive, legislative, and judicial powers so these three branches could exercise checks upon one another.

A fourth inspired principle is in the cluster of vital guarantees of individual rights and specific limits on government authority in the Bill of Rights, adopted by amendment just three years after the Constitution went into force. A Bill of Rights was not new. Here the inspiration was in the practical implementation of principles pioneered in England, beginning with the Magna Carta. The writers of the Constitution were familiar with these because some of the colonial charters had such guarantees.

Without a Bill of Rights, America could not have served as the host nation for the Restoration of the gospel, which began just three decades later. There was divine inspiration in the original provision that there should be no religious test for public office,[6] but the addition of the religious freedom and antiestablishment guarantees in the First Amendment was vital. We also see divine inspiration in the First Amendment's freedoms of speech and press and in the personal protections in other amendments, such as for criminal prosecutions.

Fifth and finally, I see divine inspiration in the vital purpose of the entire Constitution. We are to be governed by *law* and not by *individuals*, and our loyalty is to *the Constitution* and its principles and processes, not to any *office holder*. In this way, all persons are to be equal before the law. These principles block the autocratic ambitions that have corrupted democracy in some countries. They also mean that none of the three branches of government should be dominant over the others or prevent the others from performing their proper constitutional functions to check one another.

III.

Despite the divinely inspired principles of the United States Constitution, when exercised by imperfect mortals their intended effects have not always been achieved. Important subjects of lawmaking, such as some laws governing family relationships, have been taken from the states by the federal government. The First Amendment guarantee of free speech has sometimes been diluted by suppression of unpopular speech. The principle of separation of powers has always been under pressure with the ebb and flow of one branch of government exercising or inhibiting the powers delegated to another.

There are other threats that undermine the inspired principles of the United States Constitution. The stature of the Constitution is diminished by efforts to substitute current societal trends as the reason for its founding, instead of liberty and self-government. The authority of the Constitution is trivialized when candidates or officials ignore its principles. The dignity and force of the Constitution is reduced by those who refer to it like a loyalty test or a political slogan, instead of its lofty status as a source of authorization for and limits on government authority.

IV.

Our belief in divine inspiration gives Latter-day Saints a unique responsibility to uphold and defend the United States Constitution and principles of constitutionalism wherever we live. We should trust in the Lord and be positive about this nation's future.

What else are faithful Latter-day Saints to do? We must pray for the Lord to guide and bless all nations and their leaders. This is part of our article of faith. Being subject to presidents or rulers[7] of course poses no obstacle to our opposing individual laws or policies. It does require that we exercise our influence civilly and peacefully within the framework of our constitutions and applicable laws. On contested issues, we should seek to moderate and unify.

There are other duties that are part of upholding the inspired Constitution. We should learn and advocate the inspired *principles* of the Constitution. We should seek out and support wise and good persons who will support those principles in their public actions.[8] We should be knowledgeable citizens who are active in making our influence felt in civic affairs.

In the United States and in other democracies, political influence is exercised by running for office (which we encourage), by voting, by financial support, by membership and service in political parties, and by ongoing communications to officials, parties, and candidates. To function well, a democracy needs all of these, but a conscientious citizen does not need to provide all of them.

There are many political issues, and no party, platform, or individual candidate can satisfy all personal preferences. Each citizen must therefore decide which issues are most important to him or her at any particular time. Then members should seek inspiration on how to exercise their influence according to their individual priorities. This process will not be easy. It may require changing party support or candidate choices, even from election to election.

Such independent actions will sometimes require voters to support candidates or political parties or platforms whose other positions they cannot approve.[9] That is one reason we encourage our members to refrain from judging one another in political matters.

We should never assert that a faithful Latter-day Saint cannot belong to a particular party or vote for a particular candidate. We teach correct principles and leave our members to choose how to prioritize and apply those principles on the issues presented from time to time. We also insist, and we ask our local leaders to insist, that political choices and affiliations not be the subject of teachings or advocacy in any of our Church meetings.

The Church of Jesus Christ of Latter-day Saints will, of course, exercise its right to endorse or oppose specific legislative proposals that we believe will impact the free exercise of religion or the essential interests of Church organizations.

I testify of the divinely inspired Constitution of the United States and pray that we who recognize the Divine Being who inspired it will always uphold and defend its great principles. In the name of Jesus Christ, amen.

Notes

1. See Mark Tushnet, "Constitution," in Michel Rosenfeld and András Sajó, eds., *The Oxford Handbook of Comparative Constitutional Law* (2012), 222. The three countries with unwritten codified constitutions are the United Kingdom, New Zealand, and Israel. Each of these has strong traditions of constitutionalism, though the governing provisions are not collected in a single document.
2. See United States Constitution, article 1, section 2.
3. J. Reuben Clark Jr., "Constitutional Government: Our Birthright Threatened," Vital Speeches of the Day, Jan. 1, 1939, 177, quoted in Martin B. Hickman, "J. Reuben Clark, Jr.: The Constitution and the Great Fundamentals," in Ray C. Hillam, ed., *By the Hands of Wise Men: Essays on the U.S. Constitution* (1979), 53. Brigham Young held a similar developmental view of the Constitution, teaching that the framers "laid the foundation, and it was for aftergenerations to rear the superstructure upon it" (*Discourses of Brigham Young*, sel. John A. Widtsoe [1954], 359).
4. These five are similar but not identical to those suggested in J. Reuben Clark Jr., *Stand Fast by Our Constitution* (1973), 7; Ezra Taft Benson, "Our Divine Constitution," *Ensign*, Nov. 1987, 4–7; and Ezra Taft Benson, "The Constitution—A Glorious Standard," *Ensign*, Sept. 1987, 6–11. See, generally, Noel B. Reynolds, "The Doctrine of an Inspired Constitution," in *By the Hands of Wise Men*, 1–28.
5. United States Constitution, amendment 10.
6. See United States Constitution, article 6.
7. See Articles of Faith 1:12.
8. See Doctrine and Covenants 98:10.
9. See David B. Magleby, "The Necessity of Political Parties and the Importance of Compromise," *BYU Studies*, vol. 54, no. 4 (2015), 7–23.

"BEHOLD! I AM A GOD OF MIRACLES"

ELDER RONALD A. RASBAND
Of the Quorum of the Twelve Apostles

My dear brothers and sisters, what a privilege it is to stand before you today. United with those who have already addressed this conference, I testify to you that Jesus Christ lives. He directs His Church; He speaks to His prophet, President Russell M. Nelson, and He loves all Heavenly Father's children.

On this Easter Sunday we commemorate the Resurrection of Jesus Christ, our Savior and Redeemer,[1] the Mighty God, the Prince of Peace.[2] His Atonement, culminating with His Resurrection after three days in a borrowed tomb, stands as the greatest miracle in human history. "For behold," He pronounced, "I am God; and I am a God of miracles."[3]

"Have miracles ceased because Christ hath ascended into heaven, and hath sat down on the right hand of God?"[4] the prophet Mormon asks in the Book of Mormon. He answers, "Nay; neither have angels ceased to minister unto the children of men."[5]

Following the Crucifixion, an angel of the Lord appeared to Mary and a few other women who had gone to the tomb to anoint the body of Jesus. The angel said:

"Why seek ye the living among the dead?"[6]

"He is not here: for he is risen."[7]

The Book of Mormon prophet Abinadi proclaimed of that miracle:

"If Christ had not risen from the dead, . . . there could have been no resurrection.

"But there is a resurrection, therefore the grave hath no victory, and the sting of death is swallowed up in Christ."[8]

The miraculous acts of Jesus Christ caused the early disciples to exclaim: "What manner of man is this! for he commandeth even the winds and water, and they obey him."[9]

As the early Apostles followed Jesus Christ and heard Him teach the gospel, they witnessed many miracles. They saw that "the blind receive their sight, and the lame walk, the lepers are cleansed, and the deaf hear, the dead are raised up, and the poor have the gospel preached to them."[10]

Miracles, signs, and wonders abound among followers of Jesus Christ today, in your lives and in mine. Miracles are divine acts, manifestations and expressions of God's limitless power, and an affirmation that He is "the same yesterday, today, and forever."[11] Jesus Christ, who created the seas, can calm them; He who gave sight to the blind can lift our sights to heaven; He who cleansed the lepers can mend our infirmities; He who healed the impotent man can call for us to rise up with "Come, follow me."[12]

Many of you have witnessed miracles, more than you realize. They may seem small in comparison to Jesus raising the dead. But the magnitude does not distinguish a miracle, only that it came from God. Some suggest that miracles are simply coincidences or sheer luck. But the prophet Nephi condemned those who would "put down the power and miracles of God, and preach up unto themselves their own wisdom and their own learning, that they may get gain."[13]

Miracles are wrought by divine power by Him who is "mighty to save."[14] Miracles are extensions of God's eternal plan; miracles are a lifeline from heaven to earth.

Last fall Sister Rasband and I were on our way to Goshen, Utah, for a worldwide Face to Face event being broadcast to over 600,000 people in 16 different languages.[15] The program was to focus on the events of the Restoration of the gospel of Jesus Christ, with questions submitted by young adults from around the world. Sister Rasband and I had personally reviewed the questions; they gave us the opportunity to testify of Joseph Smith as a prophet of God, the power of revelation in our lives, the ongoing Restoration of the gospel of Jesus Christ, and the truths and commandments that we treasure. Many listening today were part of that miraculous event.

Initially the broadcast was to originate in the Sacred Grove in upstate New York, where, as Joseph Smith testified: "I saw two Personages, whose brightness and glory defy all description, standing above me in the air. One of them spake unto me, calling me by name and said, pointing to the other—*This is My Beloved Son. Hear Him!*[16] That, brothers and sisters, was a miracle.

The worldwide pandemic forced us to relocate the broadcast to Goshen, Utah, where The Church of Jesus Christ of Latter-day Saints has re-created, for filming, a section of old Jerusalem. Sister Rasband and I were within a few miles of Goshen that Sunday evening when we saw thick smoke coming from the direction of our destination. Wildfires were blazing in the area, and we worried the broadcast might be at risk. Sure enough, at 20 minutes to 6:00, our broadcast time, the power in the entire complex went out. No power! No broadcast. There was one generator that some thought we might be able to power up, but there was no assurance it could sustain the sophisticated equipment at hand.

All of us on the program, including narrators, musicians, and technicians—even 20 young adults from our own extended family—were fully invested in what was to take place. I stepped away from their tears and confusion and pleaded with the Lord for a miracle. "Heavenly Father," I prayed, "I have rarely asked for a miracle, but I am asking for one now. This meeting must happen for all our young adults around the world. We need the power to go on if it be Thy will."

Seven minutes after 6:00, as quickly as the power had gone out, it came back on. Everything started working, from the music and microphones to the videos and all the transmission equipment. We were off and running. We had experienced a miracle.

As Sister Rasband and I were in the car returning home later that evening, President and Sister Nelson texted us with this message: "Ron, we want you to know that as soon as we heard the power was out, we prayed for a miracle."

In latter-day scripture it is written, "For I, the Lord, have put forth my hand to exert the powers of heaven; ye cannot see it now, yet a little while and ye shall see it, and know that I am, and that I will come and reign with my people."[17]

That is exactly what happened. The Lord had put forth His hand, and the power came on.

Miracles are worked through the power of faith, as President Nelson so powerfully taught us in the last session. The prophet Moroni exhorted the people, "If there be no faith among the children of men God can do no miracle among them; wherefore, he showed not himself until after their faith."

He continued:

"Behold, it was the faith of Alma and Amulek that caused the prison to tumble to the earth.

"Behold, it was the faith of Nephi and Lehi that wrought the change upon the Lamanites, that they were baptized with fire and with the Holy Ghost.

"Behold, it was the faith of Ammon and his brethren which wrought so great a miracle among the Lamanites. . . .

"And neither at any time hath any wrought miracles until after their faith; wherefore they first believed in the Son of God."[18]

I could add to that sequence of scriptures, "It was the faith of earnest young adult performers, broadcast professionals, Church leaders and members, an apostle, and a prophet of God that sought so great a miracle that the power was restored to a remote movie set in Goshen, Utah."

Miracles can come as answers to prayer. They are not always what we ask for or what we expect, but when we trust in the Lord, He will be there, and He will be right. He will suit the miracle to the moment we need it.

The Lord performs miracles to remind us of His power, His love for us, His reach from the heavens to our mortal experience, and His desire to teach of that which is of most worth. "He that hath faith in me to be healed," He said to the Saints in 1831, and the promise continues today, "and is not appointed unto death, shall be healed."[19] There are laws decreed in the heavens, and we are always subject to them.

There are times we hope for a miracle to heal a loved one, to reverse an unjust act, or to soften the heart of a bitter or disillusioned soul. Looking at things through mortal eyes, we want the Lord to intervene, to fix what is broken. Through faith, the miracle will come, though not necessarily on our timetable or with the resolution we desired. Does that mean we are less than faithful or do not merit His intervention? No. We are beloved of the Lord. He gave His life for us, and His Atonement continues to release us from burdens and sin as we repent and draw close to Him.

The Lord has reminded us, "Neither are your ways my ways."[20] He offers, "Come unto me, all ye that labour and are heavy laden, and I will give you rest"[21]—rest from worry, disappointment, fear, disobedience, concern for loved ones, for lost or broken dreams. Peace amidst confusion or sorrow is a miracle. Remember the Lord's words: "Did I not speak peace to your mind concerning the matter? What greater witness can you have than from God?"[22] The miracle is that Jesus Christ, the Great Jehovah, the Son of the Highest, is responding with peace.

Just as He appeared to Mary in the garden, calling her by name, He calls to us to exercise our faith. Mary was looking to serve Him and care for Him. His Resurrection was not what she expected, but it was according to the great plan of happiness.

"Come down from the cross,"[23] the crowd of nonbelievers jeered at Him on Calvary. He could have performed such a miracle. But He knew the end from the beginning, and He intended to be faithful to His Father's plan. That example should not be lost on us.

To us in times of trial He has said, "Behold the wounds which pierced my side, and also the prints of the nails in my hands and feet; be faithful, keep my commandments, and ye shall inherit the kingdom of heaven."[24] That, brothers and sisters, is the miracle promised to us all.

On this Easter Sunday, as we celebrate the miracle of our Lord's Resurrection, as an Apostle of Jesus Christ I humbly pray that you will feel the power of the Redeemer in your life, that your appeals to our Heavenly Father will be answered with the love and commitment Jesus Christ demonstrated throughout His ministry. I pray that you may stand steadfast and faithful in all that is to come.

And I bless you that miracles will attend you as we experienced in Goshen—if it be the Lord's will. Look for these heaven-sent blessings in your life as you "seek this Jesus of whom the prophets and apostles have written, that the grace of God the Father, and also the Lord Jesus Christ, and the Holy Ghost, which beareth record of them, may be and abide in you forever."[25] In the name of Jesus Christ, amen.

Notes

1. See Job 19:25.
2. See Isaiah 9:6.
3. 2 Nephi 27:23.
4. Moroni 7:27.
5. Moroni 7:29.
6. Luke 24:5.
7. Matthew 28:6.
8. Mosiah 16:7–8.
9. Luke 8:25.
10. Matthew 11:5.
11. Moroni 10:19.
12. Luke 18:22.
13. 2 Nephi 26:20.
14. Doctrine and Covenants 133:47.
15. Per Michael Madsen, Jan. 11, 2021.
16. Joseph Smith—History 1:17.
17. Doctrine and Covenants 84:119.
18. Ether 12:12–15, 18.
19. Doctrine and Covenants 42:48.
20. Isaiah 55:8.
21. Matthew 11:28.
22. Doctrine and Covenants 6:23.
23. Matthew 27:40.
24. Doctrine and Covenants 6:37.
25. Ether 12:41.

LIGHT CLEAVETH UNTO LIGHT

ELDER TIMOTHY J. DYCHES
Of the Seventy

My dear brothers and sisters, I rejoice with you on this blessed Easter Sunday in contemplating the glorious light that dawned on the earth with the Resurrection of our Lord and Savior, Jesus Christ.

During His mortal ministry, Jesus declared, "I am the light of the world: he that followeth me shall not walk in darkness, but shall have the light of life."[1] The Spirit of Christ "is in all things [and] giveth life to all things."[2] It conquers the darkness that otherwise would surround us.

Years ago, in search of adventure, my two sons and I accompanied a Young Men group to the Moaning Cavern, so named for a sound that at one time echoed out of its mouth. The cavern is a chimney cave which opens into a 180-foot-deep (55 m) vertical chamber, the largest single-cave chamber in California.

There are only two ways down: the safe circular staircase or rappelling to the cavern's floor; my sons and I chose to rappel. My older son went first, while my younger son and I purposely went last so that we would descend together.

After our guides instructed and secured us with harness and belay gear to a strong rope, we inched backward until we stood on a small ledge and gathered our confidence, as this was the last place to turn around and the last place we could see any sunlight from the mouth of the cave.

Our next step backwards plunged us into a cathedral cavern so tall and wide that it could swallow the Statue of Liberty. There we dangled in a slow spin as our eyes adjusted to the relative darkness. As we continued our descent, the glow of electric lights illuminated an amazing wall of glistening stalagmites and stalactites.

Without warning, the lights suddenly went completely out. Suspended above the abyss, we were engulfed in a darkness so profound that we could not even see our hands on the ropes in front of us. A voice instantly called out, "Dad, Dad, are you there?"

"I'm here, Son; I'm right here," I responded.

The unexpected loss of light was designed to show that without electricity, the darkness of the cavern was impenetrable. It succeeded; we "felt" the darkness. When the lights did return, the darkness instantly surrendered, as darkness must always surrender, to even the faintest light. My sons and I have been left with a memory of a darkness we had never known, a greater appreciation for light we will never forget, and the assurance that we are never all alone in the dark.

Our descent into that cavern in some ways parallels our journey through mortality. We departed from the glorious light of heaven and descended through a veil of forgetfulness to a darkened world. Our Heavenly Father did not abandon us to darkness but promised us light for our journey through His Beloved Son, Jesus Christ.

We know that sunlight is vital to all life on earth. Equally vital to our spiritual life is the light that emanates from our Savior. In His perfect love, God grants the Light of Christ to every person "that cometh into the world"[3] that they may "know good from evil"[4] and be prompted "to do good continually."[5] That light, revealing itself through what we often call our conscience, beckons us ever to act and be better, to be our best self.

As we intensify our faith in Christ, we receive light in intensifying measure until it dispels all darkness that might gather around us. "That which is of God is light; and he that receiveth light, and continueth in God, receiveth more light; and that light groweth brighter and brighter until the perfect day."[6]

The Light of Christ prepares us to receive the ministering influence of the Holy Ghost, which is "the convincing power of God . . . of the truth of the Gospel."[7] The third member of the Godhead, the Holy Ghost "is a personage of Spirit."[8] The greatest source of light that Heavenly Father imparts to you in mortality comes through the Holy Ghost, whose influence "shall enlighten your mind [and] fill your soul with joy."[9]

In The Church of Jesus Christ of Latter-day Saints, through restored priesthood authority, you are baptized by immersion for the remission of sins. Then hands are laid upon your head and this wonderful, "unspeakable gift"[10] of the Holy Ghost is bestowed upon you.

Thereafter, when your desires and actions are centered on the covenant path, the Holy Ghost, as a light within you, will reveal and testify of truth,[11] warn of danger, comfort[12] and cleanse,[13] and provide peace[14] to your soul.

Because "light cleaveth unto light,"[15] the constant companionship of the Holy Ghost will lead you to make choices that will tend to keep you in the light; conversely, choices made without the Holy Ghost's influence will tend to lead you into shadows and darkness. Elder Robert D. Hales taught: "When light is present, darkness is vanquished and must depart. . . . When the spiritual light of the Holy Ghost is present, the darkness of Satan departs."[16]

May I suggest that perhaps this is the time to ask yourself: Do I have that light in my life? If not, when was the last time I did?

Just as sunlight daily bathes the earth to renew and sustain life, you can daily brighten the light within you when you choose to follow Him—Jesus Christ.

A drop of sunshine is added every time you seek God in prayer; study the scriptures to "hear Him";[17] act on guidance and revelation from our living prophets; and obey and keep the commandments to "walk in all the ordinances of the Lord."[18]

You will invite spiritual sunlight into your soul and peace into your life each time you repent. As you partake of the sacrament every week to take the Savior's name upon you, to always remember Him and keep His commandments, His light will shine within you.

There is sunshine in your soul every time you share the gospel and bear your testimony. Every time you serve one another as the Savior did, His warmth is felt in your heart. Heavenly Father's light always resides within His holy temple and upon all who present themselves in the house of the Lord. His light in you is enhanced with your acts of kindness, patience, forgiveness, and charity and shows itself in your happy countenance. On the other hand, we walk in shadows when we are too quick to anger or too slow to forgive. "As you keep your face towards the sunshine, the shadows cannot help but fall behind you."[19]

As you live to merit the companionship of the Holy Ghost, you truly "increase your spiritual capacity to receive revelation."[20]

Life presents challenges and setbacks, and we all must face some dark days and storms. Through it all, if we "let God prevail in our lives,"[21] the light of the Holy Ghost will reveal that there is purpose and meaning in our trials, that they will ultimately transform us into better, more complete individuals with a firmer faith and brighter hope in Christ, knowing that God was there with us in our dark days all along. As President Russell M. Nelson has counseled, "The increasing darkness that accompanies tribulation makes the light of Jesus Christ shine ever brighter."[22]

Seasons of our lives can take us to places both unexpected and undesirable. If sin has led you there, pull back the curtain of darkness and begin now to humbly approach your Heavenly Father with a broken heart and a contrite spirit and repent. He will hear your earnest prayer. With courage today, "draw near unto [Him] and [He] will draw near unto you."[23] You are never beyond the healing power of the Atonement of Jesus Christ.

I come from goodly parents and from faithful ancestors who responded to the light of Jesus Christ and His gospel, and it blessed their lives and the generations that have followed with spiritual resilience. My dad often talked about his father, Milo T Dyches, and shared how his faith in God was a light to him day and night. Grandpa was a forest ranger and often rode alone in the mountains, entrusting his life without question to God's direction and care.

Late one fall, Grandpa was alone in the high mountains. Winter had already shown its face when he saddled one of his favorite horses, old Prince, and rode to a sawmill to scale and measure logs before they could be sawed into lumber.

At dusk, he finished his work and climbed back into the saddle.

By then, the temperature had plummeted, and a fierce winter snowstorm was engulfing the mountain. With neither light nor path to guide him, he turned Prince in a direction he thought would lead them back to the ranger station.

After traveling miles in the dark, Prince slowed, then stopped. Grandpa repeatedly urged Prince forward, but the horse refused. With blinding snow swirling around them, Grandpa realized he needed God's help. As he had done throughout his life, he humbly "ask[ed] in faith, nothing wavering."[24] A still, small voice answered, "Milo, give Prince his head." Grandpa obeyed, and as he lightened his hold on the reins, Prince swung around and plodded off in a different direction. Hours later, Prince again halted and lowered his head. Through the driving snow, Grandpa saw that they had safely arrived at the gate of the ranger station.

With the morning sun, Grandpa retraced the faint tracks of Prince in the snow. He drew a deep breath when he found where he had given Prince his head: it was the very brink of a lofty mountain cliff, where a single step forward would have plunged both horse and rider to their deaths in the rugged rocks below.

Based on that experience and many others, Grandpa counseled, "The best and greatest partner you will ever have is your Father in Heaven." When my dad would relate Grandpa's story, I remember that he would quote from the scriptures:

"Trust in the Lord with all thine heart; and lean not unto thine own understanding.

"In all thy ways acknowledge him, and he shall direct thy paths."[25]

I testify that Jesus Christ is the everlasting light that "shineth in darkness."[26] There is no darkness that can ever suppress, extinguish, overpower, or defeat that light. Our Heavenly Father freely offers that light to you. You are never alone. He hears and answers every prayer. He has "called you out of darkness into his marvellous light."[27] When you ask, "Father, Father, are You there?" He will always reply, "I'm here, child of mine; I'm right here."

I bear witness that Jesus Christ fulfilled Heavenly Father's plan as our Savior and our Redeemer;[28] He is our light, our life, and our way. His light will never dim;[29] His glory will never cease; His love for you is eternal—yesterday, today, and forever. In the name of Jesus Christ, amen.

Notes

1. John 8:12.
2. Doctrine and Covenants 88:13.
3. Doctrine and Covenants 93:2.
4. Moroni 7:16.
5. Moroni 7:13.
6. Doctrine and Covenants 50:24.
7. Wilford Woodruff, in *History of the Church*, 4:555.
8. Doctrine and Covenants 130:22.
9. Doctrine and Covenants 11:13.
10. Doctrine and Covenants 121:26.
11. See John 16:13; Jacob 4:13; Moroni 10:5.
12. See John 14:16; Moroni 8:26.
13. See 2 Nephi 31:17.
14. See Doctrine and Covenants 36:2.
15. Doctrine and Covenants 88:40.
16. Robert D. Hales, "Out of Darkness into His Marvelous Light," *Ensign*, May 2002, 70; *Liahona*, July 2002, 78.
17. Russell M. Nelson, "Hear Him," *Ensign* or *Liahona*, May 2020, 89.
18. Doctrine and Covenants 136:4.
19. Unknown author.
20. Russell M. Nelson, "Revelation for the Church, Revelation for Our Lives," *Ensign* or *Liahona*, May 2018, 96.
21. Russell M. Nelson "Let God Prevail," *Ensign* or *Liahona*, Nov. 2020, 95.
22. Russell M. Nelson, "Hear Him," 88.
23. Doctrine and Covenants 88:63.
24. James 1:6.
25. Proverbs 3:5–6.
26. John 1:5.
27. 1 Peter 2:9.
28. See Doctrine and Covenants 93:9.
29. See 2 Nephi 10:14.

WHY THE COVENANT PATH

ELDER D. TODD CHRISTOFFERSON
Of the Quorum of the Twelve Apostles

Throughout his ministry, President Russell M. Nelson has studied and taught of God's covenants with His children. He is himself a shining example of one who walks the covenant path. In his first message as President of the Church, President Nelson stated:

"Your commitment to follow the Savior by making covenants with Him and then keeping these covenants will open the door to every spiritual blessing and privilege available to men, women, and children everywhere.

". . . The ordinances of the temple and the covenants you make there are key to strengthening your life, your marriage and family, and your ability to resist the attacks of the adversary. Your worship in the temple and your service there for your ancestors will bless you with increased personal revelation and peace and will fortify your commitment to stay on the covenant path."[1]

What is the covenant path? It is the one path that leads to the celestial kingdom of God. We embark upon the path at the gate of baptism and then "press forward with a steadfastness in Christ, having a perfect brightness of hope, and a love of God and of all men [the two great commandments] . . . to the end."[2] In the course of the covenant path (which, by the way, extends beyond mortality), we receive all the ordinances and covenants pertaining to salvation and exaltation.

Our overarching covenant commitment is to do God's will "and to be obedient to his commandments in all things that he shall command us."[3] Following the principles and commandments of the gospel of Jesus Christ day by day is the happiest and most satisfying course in life. For one thing, a person avoids a great many problems and regrets. Let me use a sports analogy. In tennis, there is something called unforced errors. These are things such as hitting a playable ball into the net or double-faulting when serving. Unforced errors are considered the result of a player's blunder rather than be-ing caused by the opponent's skill.

Too often our problems or challenges are self-inflicted, the result of poor choices, or, we could say, the result of "unforced errors." When we are diligently pursuing the covenant path, we quite nat-urally avoid many "unforced errors." We sidestep the various forms of addiction. We do not fall into the ditch of dishonest conduct. We cross over the abyss of immorality and infidelity. We bypass the people and things that, even if popular, would jeopardize our phys-ical and spiritual well-being. We avoid the choices that harm or dis-advantage others and instead acquire the habits of self-discipline and service.[4]

Elder J. Golden Kimball is purported to have said, "I may not have [always] walked the straight and narrow, but I [try] to cross it as often as I [can]."[5] In a more serious moment, I am sure Brother Kimball would agree that staying on, not just crossing, the covenant path is our greatest hope for avoiding *avoidable* misery on the one hand and successfully dealing with the *unavoidable* woes of life on the other.

Some might say, "I can make good choices with or without bap-tism; I don't need covenants to be an honorable and successful per-son." Indeed, there are many who, while not on the covenant path themselves, act in a way that mirrors the choices and contributions of those who are on the path. You might say they reap the blessings of walking a "covenant-consistent" path. What, then, is the differ-ence of the covenant path?

Actually, the difference is uniquely and eternally significant. It includes the nature of our obedience, the character of God's com-mitment to us, the divine help we receive, the blessings tied to gathering as a covenant people, and most importantly, our eternal inheritance.

Committed Obedience

First is the nature of our obedience to God. More than simply having good intentions, we solemnly commit to live by every word that proceeds forth from the mouth of God. In this, we follow the example of Jesus Christ, who, by being baptized, "showeth unto the children of men that, according to the flesh he humbleth himself before the Father, and witnesseth unto the Father that he would be obedient unto him in keeping his commandments."[6]

With covenants, we are intent on more than just avoiding mistakes or being prudent in our decisions. We feel accountable to God for our choices and our lives. We take upon us the name of Christ. We are focused on Christ—on being valiant in the testimony of Jesus and on developing the character of Christ.

With covenants, obedience to gospel principles becomes rooted in our very soul. I am familiar with a couple where, at the time of their marriage, the wife was not active in the Church and the husband had never been a member of the Church. I will refer to them as Mary and John, not their real names. As children began to enter the picture, Mary felt keenly the need to raise them, as the scripture says, "in the nurture and admonition of the Lord."[7] John was supportive. Mary made some important sacrifices to be at home to teach the gospel on a consistent basis. She ensured that the family took full advantage of Church worship and activity. Mary and John became exemplary parents, and their children (all energetic boys) grew in faith and devotion to gospel principles and standards.

John's parents, the boys' grandparents, were pleased with the wholesome lives and achievements of their grandsons, but because of some antagonism toward the Church, they wanted to attribute this success exclusively to the parenting skills of John and Mary. John, although not a member of the Church, did not let that assessment go unchallenged. He insisted that they were witnessing the fruits of gospel teachings—what his sons were experiencing in church as well as what was happening at home.

John himself was being influenced by the Spirit, by the love and example of his wife, and by the urgings of his sons. In due course, he was baptized, much to the joy of ward members and friends.

While life has not been without challenges for them and their sons, Mary and John wholeheartedly affirm that it is in fact the gospel covenant that is at the root of their blessings. They have seen the Lord's words to Jeremiah fulfilled in the lives of their children as well as their own: "I will put my law in their inward parts, and write it in their hearts; and will be their God, and they shall be my people."[8]

Bound to God

A second unique aspect of the covenant path is our relationship with Deity. The covenants God offers to His children do more than guide us. They bind us to Him, and, bound to Him, we can overcome all things.[9]

I once read an article by a poorly informed newspaper reporter who explained that the way we perform baptisms for the dead is to immerse rolls of microfilm in water. Then all those whose names appear on the microfilm are considered baptized. That approach would be efficient, but it ignores the infinite worth of each soul and the critical importance of a personal covenant with God.

"[Jesus] said . . . : Enter ye in at the strait gate; for strait is the gate, and narrow is the way that leads to life, and few there be that find it."[10] Figuratively speaking, this gate is so narrow that it allows only one to enter at a time. Each one makes an individual commitment to God and in return receives from Him a personal covenant, by name, that he or she can rely on implicitly in time and eternity. With the ordinances and covenants, "the power of godliness is manifest" in our lives.[11]

Divine Help

This leads us to consideration of a third special blessing of the covenant path. God provides an almost incomprehensible gift to help covenant-makers be covenant-keepers: the gift of the Holy Ghost. This gift is the right to the constant companionship, protection, and guidance of the Holy Spirit.[12] Also known as the Comforter, the Holy Spirit "filleth with hope and perfect love."[13] He "knoweth all things, and beareth record of the Father and of the Son,"[14] whose witnesses we commit to be.[15]

On the covenant path we also find the essential blessings of forgiveness and cleansing from sin. This is help that can come only through divine grace, administered by the Holy Ghost. "Now this is the commandment," says the Lord, "Repent, all ye ends of the earth, and come unto me and be baptized in my name, that ye may be sanctified by the reception of the Holy Ghost, that ye may stand spotless before me at the last day."[16]

Gather with the Covenant People

Fourth, those pursuing the covenant path also find singular blessings in various divinely appointed gatherings. Prophecies of a literal gathering of the long-dispersed tribes of Israel to the lands of their inheritance are found throughout the scriptures.[17] The fulfillment of those prophecies and promises is now underway with the gathering of the covenant people into the Church, the kingdom of God on earth. President Nelson explains, "When we speak of the *gathering*, we are simply saying this fundamental truth: every one of our Heavenly Father's children . . . deserves to hear the message of the restored gospel of Jesus Christ."[18]

The Lord commands members of The Church of Jesus Christ of Latter-day Saints to "arise and shine forth, that thy light may be a standard for the nations; . . . that the gathering together upon the land of Zion, and upon her stakes, may be for a defense, and for a refuge from the storm, and from wrath when it shall be poured out without mixture upon the whole earth."[19]

There is also a weekly gathering of the covenant people to the house of prayer on the Lord's day, that we may "more fully keep [ourselves] unspotted from the world."[20] It is a gathering to partake of sacramental bread and water in remembrance of the Atonement of Jesus Christ and a time "to fast and to pray, and to speak one with another concerning the welfare of [our] souls."[21] As a teenager, I was the only member of the Church in my high school class. I enjoyed the association of many good friends in school, yet I found that I relied heavily on this Sabbath gathering each week to refresh and renew me spiritually, and even physically. How keenly we have felt the loss of this regular covenant gathering during the current pandemic, and how eagerly we anticipate the time when we can come together again as before.

The covenant people also gather to the temple, the house of the Lord, to obtain the ordinances, blessings, and revelation uniquely available there. The Prophet Joseph Smith taught: "What was the object of gathering the . . . people of God in any age of the world? . . . The main object was to build unto the Lord a house whereby He could reveal unto His people the ordinances of His house and the glories of His kingdom, and teach the people the way of salvation; for there are certain ordinances and principles that, when they are taught and practiced, must be done in a place or house built for that purpose."[22]

Inherit the Covenant Promises

Finally, it is only in pursuing the covenant path that we inherit the blessings of Abraham, Isaac, and Jacob, the ultimate blessings of salvation and exaltation that only God can give.[23]

Scriptural references to the covenant people often mean literal descendants of Abraham or the "house of Israel." But the covenant people also include all who receive the gospel of Jesus Christ.[24] Paul explained:

"For as many of you as have been baptized into Christ have put on Christ. . . .

"And if ye be Christ's, then are ye Abraham's seed, and heirs according to the promise."[25]

Those who are loyal to their covenants "shall come forth in the resurrection of the just."[26] They are "made perfect through Jesus the mediator of the new covenant. . . . These are they whose bodies are celestial, whose glory is that of the sun, even the glory of God, the highest of all."[27] "Wherefore, all things are theirs, whether life or death, or things present, or things to come, all are theirs and they are Christ's, and Christ is God's."[28]

Let us heed the prophet's call to stay on the covenant path. Nephi saw us and our time and recorded, "I, Nephi, beheld the power of the Lamb of God, that it descended upon the saints of the church of the Lamb, and upon the covenant people of the Lord, who were scattered upon all the face of the earth; and they were armed with righteousness and with the power of God in great glory."[29]

With Nephi, "my soul delighteth in the covenants of the Lord."[30] On this Easter Sunday, I bear testimony of Jesus Christ, whose Resurrection is our hope and the assurance of all that is promised on and at the end of the covenant path. In the name of Jesus Christ, amen.

Notes

1. Russell M. Nelson, "As We Go Forward Together," *Ensign* or *Liahona*, Apr. 2018, 7.
2. 2 Nephi 31:20. The covenant path was established from the beginning with Adam and Eve (see Moses 6:50–68).
3. Mosiah 5:5. As Alma the Elder expressed, "If this be the desire of your hearts, what have you against being baptized in the name of the Lord, as a witness before him that ye have entered into a covenant with him, that ye will serve him and keep his commandments, that he may pour out his Spirit more abundantly upon you?" (Mosiah 18:10).
4. For a scriptural example, see Alma 1:29–32.
5. In Eric A. Eliason, *The J. Golden Kimball Stories* (2007), 78.
6. See 2 Nephi 31:6–7.
7. Ephesians 6:4; see also Enos 1:1.
8. Jeremiah 31:33.
9. See John 16:33.
10. 3 Nephi 27:33; see also Matthew 7:14.
11. See Doctrine and Covenants 84:20.
12. See Bible Dictionary, "Holy Ghost."
13. Moroni 8:26.
14. Doctrine and Covenants 42:17.
15. See Mosiah 18:9.
16. 3 Nephi 27:20; see also 2 Nephi 31:17.
17. See, for example, Isaiah 5:26–29 (2 Nephi 15:26–28); Isaiah 54:7; Jeremiah 16:14–16; 2 Nephi 29:14; 3 Nephi 29:1; Articles of Faith 1:10. The coming forth of the Book of Mormon is a sign that the Lord has begun to fulfill His covenant with the house of Israel, including "their restoration to the lands of their inheritance" (3 Nephi 29:1; see also 3 Nephi 21:1–7). The Book of Mormon is also the instrument used to accomplish that gathering (see 3 Nephi 16:4–8).
18. Russell M. Nelson, "Hope of Israel" (worldwide youth devotional, June 3, 2018), HopeofIsrael.ChurchofJesusChrist.org; see also Russell M. Nelson, "Covenants," *Ensign* or *Liahona*, Nov. 2011, 86–89.
19. Doctrine and Covenants 115:5–6.
20. Doctrine and Covenants 59:9.
21. Moroni 6:5.
22. *Teachings of Presidents of the Church: Joseph Smith* (2007), 416.
23. See Bible Dictionary, "Abraham, covenant of"; Abraham 2:11.
24. The Book of Mormon is sent to the Gentiles, "that they may repent and come unto me and be baptized in my name and know of the true points of my doctrine, that they may be numbered among my people, O house of Israel" (3 Nephi 21:6).
25. Galatians 3:27, 29; see also Abraham 2:10. At the same time, even those who may be the literal descendants or seed of Abraham forfeit their legacy as part of the Lord's chosen people unless they accept Jesus Christ. "For it shall come to pass, saith the Father, that at that day whosoever

will not repent and come unto my Beloved Son, them will I cut off from among my people, O house of Israel" (3 Nephi 21:20).

26. Doctrine and Covenants 76:65.
27. Doctrine and Covenants 76:69–70.
28. Doctrine and Covenants 76:59.
29. 1 Nephi 14:14.
30. 2 Nephi 11:5.

THE GOSPEL LIGHT OF TRUTH AND LOVE

ELDER ALAN R. WALKER
Of the Seventy

The beautiful Latter-day Saint hymn "Hark, All Ye Nations!" unmistakably captures the enthusiasm and exhilaration of the fulness of the gospel going to all the world. In this hymn we sing:

> *Hark, all ye nations! Hear heaven's voice*
> *Thru ev'ry land that all may rejoice!*
> *Angels of glory shout the refrain:*
> *Truth is restored again!*[1]

Louis F. Mönch, the author of this jubilant text, was a German convert who wrote the inspired words for the hymn while living in Switzerland during his full-time missionary service in Europe.[2] The joy that springs from witnessing the global impact of the Restoration is clearly articulated in the following words of the hymn:

> *Searching in darkness, nations have wept;*
> *Watching for dawn, their vigil they've kept.*
> *All now rejoice; the long night is o'er.*
> *Truth is on earth once more!*[3]

Thanks to the commencing of the ongoing Restoration just over 200 years ago, "the gospel light of truth and love"[4] now shines brightly throughout the earth. The Prophet Joseph learned in 1820, and millions more have since learned, that God "giveth to all men liberally, and upbraideth not."[5]

Shortly after the organization of the Church in this last dispensation, the Lord spoke to Joseph Smith and manifested His abounding love for us when He said:

"Wherefore, I the Lord, knowing the calamity which should come upon the inhabitants of the earth, called upon my servant Joseph Smith, Jun., and spake unto him from heaven, and gave him commandments; . . .

"That mine everlasting covenant might be established;

"That the fulness of my gospel might be proclaimed by the weak and the simple unto the ends of the world."[6]

Soon after this revelation was received, missionaries began to be called and sent to many nations of the world. Just as the prophet Nephi anticipated, the message of the restored gospel began to be preached "among all nations, kindreds, tongues, and people."[7]

"The Church of Jesus Christ of Latter-day Saints was formally organized in a small log cabin in upstate New York in 1830.

"It took 117 years—until 1947—for the Church to grow from the initial six members to one million. Missionaries were a feature of the Church from its earliest days, fanning out to Native American lands, to Canada and, in 1837, beyond the North American continent to England. Not long after, missionaries were working on the European continent and as far away as India and the Pacific Islands.

"The two-million-member mark was reached just 16 years later, in 1963, and the three-million mark in eight years more."[8]

Highlighting the rapid growth of the Church, President Russell M. Nelson recently said: "Today, the Lord's work in The Church of Jesus Christ of Latter-day Saints is moving forward at an accelerated pace. The Church will have an unprecedented, unparalleled future."[9]

The Restoration of the fulness of the gospel of Jesus Christ, the organization of the Lord's living Church on the earth again, and its remarkable growth since then have made the blessings of the priesthood available throughout the earth. Sacred ordinances and covenants that bind us to God and set us on the covenant path clearly manifest "the power of godliness."[10] As we participate in these sacred ordinances for the living and for the dead, we gather Israel on both sides of the veil and prepare the earth for the Second Coming of the Savior.

In April 1973, my parents and I traveled from our native Argentina to be sealed in the temple. Since there were no temples in all of Latin America at the time, we flew more than 6,000 miles (9,700 km) each way to be sealed in the Salt Lake Temple. Although

I was just two years of age at the time and do not recall the entirety of that special experience, three very distinct images from that trip were fixed in my mind and have remained ever since.

First, I recall being placed close to the airplane's window and seeing the white clouds below.

Those beautiful, bright clouds endure in my mind as if they had been gigantic cotton balls.

Another image that has remained in my mind is that of a few funny-looking characters at an amusement park in the Los Angeles area. Those characters are hard to forget.

But of much greater importance is this brilliant and unforgettable image:

I clearly remember being in a sacred room of the Salt Lake Temple where sealings of couples and of families are performed for time and for all eternity. I remember the beautiful altar of the temple and recall the bright sunlight shining through the room's exterior window. I felt then, and have continued to feel since, the warmth, safety, and solace of the gospel light of truth and love.

Similar feelings were reaffirmed in my heart 20 years later, when I entered the temple to be sealed once again—this time as my fiancée and I were sealed for time and for all eternity. However, on this occasion, we did not need to travel thousands of miles because the Buenos Aires Argentina Temple had since been built and dedicated, and it was just a short drive from our home.

Twenty-two years after our wedding and sealing, we had the blessing of returning to the same temple, but this time with our beautiful daughter, and we were sealed as a family for time and for all eternity.

As I've reflected upon these very sacred moments of my life, I have been overwhelmed with profound, enduring joy. I have felt and continue to feel the love of a compassionate Father in Heaven, who knows our individual needs and our heartfelt desires.

In addressing the gathering of Israel in the last days, the Lord Jehovah said, "I will put my law in their inward parts, and write it in their hearts; and will be their God, and they shall be my people."[11]

I feel eternally grateful that from my young age, the law of the Lord started to be engraved deeply in my heart through sacred ordinances in His holy house. How fundamental it is to know that He is our God, that we are His people, and that whatever circumstances surround us, if we are faithful and obey the covenants we have entered into, we can be "encircled about eternally in the arms of his love."[12]

During the women's session of general conference in October 2019, President Nelson said, "All our efforts to minister to each other, proclaim the gospel, perfect the Saints, and redeem the dead converge in the holy temple."[13]

Also, during the same general conference, President Nelson taught: "Of course, the crowning jewel of the Restoration is the holy temple. Its sacred ordinances and covenants are pivotal to preparing a people who are ready to welcome the Savior at His Second Coming."[14]

The ongoing Restoration has been marked by the building and dedication of temples at an augmented pace. As we gather on both sides of the veil, as we make sacrifices to serve and make the temple pivotal in our lives, the Lord is truly building us—He is building His covenant people.

> *Oh, how glorious from the throne above*
> *Shines the gospel light of truth and love!*
> *Bright as the sun, this heavenly ray*
> *Lights ev'ry land today.*[15]

I testify that the gospel light of truth and love shines brightly throughout the earth today. The "marvellous work and a wonder" foretold by the prophet Isaiah[16] and seen by Nephi[17] is taking place at a hastened pace, even in these challenging times. As Joseph Smith prophetically declared, "The Standard of Truth has been erected; no unhallowed hand can stop the work from progressing . . . till the purposes of God shall be accomplished, and the Great Jehovah shall say the work is done."[18]

Brothers and sisters, may we be willing and decide today to engage ourselves and our families in hearing heaven's voice, even the voice of our Savior. May we make and keep covenants with God, which will secure us firmly in the path that leads back to His presence, and may we rejoice in the blessings of the glorious light and truth of His gospel. In the name of Jesus Christ, amen.

Notes

1. "Hark, All Ye Nations!," *Hymns*, no. 264.
2. See Karen Lynn Davidson, *Our Latter-Day Hymns: The Stories and the Messages* (1988), 268–69, 413.
3. "Hark, All Ye Nations!," *Hymns*, no. 264.
4. "Hark, All Ye Nations!," *Hymns*, no. 264.
5. James 1:5.
6. Doctrine and Covenants 1:17, 22–23.
7. 2 Nephi 30:8.
8. "Growth of the Church," newsroom.ChurchofJesusChrist.org.
9. Russell M. Nelson, "The Future of the Church: Preparing the World for the Savior's Second Coming," *Ensign*, Apr. 2020, 13; *Liahona*, Apr. 2020, 7.
10. Doctrine and Covenants 84:20.
11. Jeremiah 31:33.
12. 2 Nephi 1:15.
13. Russell M. Nelson, "Spiritual Treasures," *Ensign* or *Liahona*, Nov. 2019, 79.
14. Russell M. Nelson, "Closing Remarks," *Ensign* or *Liahona*, Nov. 2019, 120.
15. "Hark, All Ye Nations!," *Hymns*, no. 264.
16. Isaiah 29:14.
17. See 2 Nephi 25:17.
18. *Teachings of Presidents of the Church: Joseph Smith* (2007), 142.

"THE PRINCIPLES OF MY GOSPEL" (DOCTRINE AND COVENANTS 42:12)

ELDER DAVID A. BEDNAR
Of the Quorum of the Twelve Apostles

In the general conference of The Church of Jesus Christ of Latter-day Saints in October 1849, Elder John Taylor of the Quorum of the Twelve Apostles was called to open the nation of France for the preaching of the gospel of Jesus Christ. His service included the editing of the first official Church periodical in that country. Elder Taylor prepared and published an article in 1851 in response to frequent questions he had been asked about the Church. And near the end of that essay, Elder Taylor recalled the following episode:

"Some years ago, in Nauvoo, a gentleman in my hearing, a member of the Legislature, asked Joseph Smith how it was that he was enabled to govern so many people, and to preserve such perfect order; remarking at the same time that it was impossible for them to do it anywhere else. Mr. Smith remarked that it was very easy to do that. 'How?' responded the gentleman; 'to us it is very difficult.' Mr. Smith replied, 'I teach them correct principles, and they govern themselves.'"[1]

I pray that the Holy Ghost will instruct and edify each of us as I emphasize the important role of principles in the restored gospel of Jesus Christ.

Principles

The Lord revealed to the Prophet Joseph Smith that "the elders, priests and teachers of this church shall teach the principles of my gospel, which are in the Bible and the Book of Mormon, in the which is the fulness of the gospel."[2] He also declared that the Latter-day Saints should "be instructed more perfectly in theory, in principle, in doctrine, in the law of the gospel, in all things that pertain unto the kingdom of God, that are expedient for you to understand."[3]

Stated succinctly, a gospel principle is a doctrinally based guideline for the righteous exercise of moral agency. Principles derive from broader gospel truths and provide direction and standards as we press forward on the covenant path.

For example, the first three Articles of Faith identify fundamental aspects of the doctrine of the restored gospel of Jesus Christ: the nature of the Godhead in the first article of faith, the effects of the Fall of Adam and Eve in the second article of faith, and the blessings made possible through the Atonement of Jesus Christ in the third article of faith.[4] And the fourth article of faith sets forth the first principles—the guidelines of exercising faith in Jesus Christ and repenting—and the first priesthood ordinances that enable the Atonement of Jesus Christ to be efficacious in our lives.[5]

The Word of Wisdom is another example of a principle as a guideline. Please note these introductory verses in section 89 of the Doctrine and Covenants:

"Given for a principle with promise, adapted to the capacity of the weak and the weakest of all saints, who are or can be called saints.

"Behold, verily, thus saith the Lord unto you: In consequence of evils and designs which do and will exist in the hearts of conspiring men in the last days, I have warned you, and forewarn you, by giving unto you this word of wisdom by revelation."[6]

The inspired instruction that follows this introduction provides enduring guidelines for both physical and spiritual well-being and testifies of specific blessings contingent upon our faithfulness to the principle.

Learning, understanding, and living gospel principles strengthen our faith in the Savior, deepen our devotion to Him, and invite a multitude of blessings and spiritual gifts into our lives. Principles of righteousness also help us to look beyond our personal preferences and self-centered desires by providing the precious perspective of eternal truth as we navigate the different circumstances, challenges, decisions, and experiences of mortality.

Contemporary Examples of Teaching Correct Principles

The statement by the Prophet Joseph Smith about teaching correct principles is perhaps one of his most frequently quoted teachings. And we find powerful examples of this inspired pattern of instruction in the pronouncements of the Lord's authorized servants today.

The Principle of Non-Distraction

President Dallin H. Oaks spoke in general conference in 1998 about Aaronic Priesthood holders' duties related to preparing and administering the sacrament. He described *the principle of non-distraction* and indicated that a holder of the Aaronic Priesthood would never want anything in his appearance or behavior to distract any member of the Church from his or her worship and renewal of covenants. President Oaks also emphasized the related principles of orderliness, cleanliness, reverence, and dignity.

Interestingly, President Oaks did not provide for the young men a lengthy list of things to do and not to do. Rather, he explained the principle with the expectation that the young men and their parents and teachers could and should use their own judgment and inspiration to follow the guideline.

He explained: "I will not suggest detailed rules, since the circumstances in various wards and branches in our worldwide Church are so different that a specific rule that seems required in one setting may be inappropriate in another. Rather, I will suggest a principle based on the doctrines. If all understand this principle and act in harmony with it, there should be little need for rules. If rules or counseling are needed in individual cases, local leaders can provide them, consistent with the doctrines and their related principles."[7]

The Principle of the Sabbath as a Sign

In the April 2015 general conference, President Russell M. Nelson taught us that "the Sabbath is a delight."[8] He also explained how he personally had come to understand a basic principle about honoring the Sabbath day:

"How do we *hallow* the Sabbath day? In my much younger years, I studied the work of others who had compiled lists of things to do and things *not* to do on the Sabbath. It wasn't until later that I learned from the scriptures that my conduct and my attitude on the Sabbath constituted a *sign* between me and my Heavenly Father. With that understanding, I no longer needed lists of dos and don'ts. When I had to make a decision whether or not an activity was appropriate for the Sabbath, I simply asked myself, '*What sign do I want to give to God?*' That question made my choices about the Sabbath day crystal clear."[9]

President Nelson's simple but powerful question emphasizes a principle that cuts through any uncertainty about what it means and what we should do to honor the Sabbath. His question summarizes a guideline and standard that can bless all of us in our varied circumstances.

The Principle of Being Willing to Let God Prevail

Six months ago in general conference, President Nelson described his personal elation as he was led to a new insight about the meaning of the word *Israel*. He told us that his soul was stirred as he learned that "the very name of *Israel* refers to a person who is *willing* to let God prevail in his or her life."[10] President Nelson then identified a number of important implications that derive from this insight.

His message about *being willing to let God prevail* is a remarkable example of teaching correct principles so that we can govern ourselves. And just as he did in his message about making the Sabbath a delight, President Nelson posed principle-based questions that serve as guides and standards for each of us.

"Are *you* willing to let God prevail in your life? Are *you* willing to let God be the most important influence in your life?"

He continued:

"Consider how such willingness could bless you. If you are

unmarried and seeking an eternal companion, your desire to be 'of Israel' will help you decide whom to date and how.

"If you are married to a companion who has broken his or her covenants, your willingness to let God prevail in your life will allow your covenants with God to remain intact. The Savior will heal your broken heart. The heavens will open as you seek to know how to move forward. You do not need to wander or wonder.

"If you have sincere questions about the gospel or the Church, as you choose to let God prevail, you will be led to find and understand the absolute, eternal truths that will guide your life and help you stay firmly on the covenant path.

"When you are faced with temptation—even if the temptation comes when you are exhausted or feeling alone or misunderstood—imagine the courage you can muster as you choose to let God prevail in your life and as you plead with Him to strengthen you.

"When your greatest desire is to let God prevail, to be part of Israel, so many decisions become easier. So many issues become nonissues! You know how best to groom yourself. You know what to watch and read, where to spend your time, and with whom to associate. You know what you want to accomplish. You know the kind of person you really want to become."[11]

Note how many crucial decisions and life experiences can be influenced by the principle of *being willing to let God prevail*: dating and marriage, gospel questions and concerns, temptation, personal grooming, what to watch and read, where to spend time, with whom to associate, and many, many more. President Nelson's inspired questions emphasize a simple principle that provides direction in every aspect of our lives and enables us to govern ourselves.

A Very Small Helm

When Joseph Smith was imprisoned in Liberty Jail, he wrote letters of instruction to Church members and leaders and reminded them that "a very large ship is benefited very much by a very small helm in the time of a storm, by being kept workways with the wind and the waves."[12]

A "helm" is a wheel or tiller and the associated equipment used to steer a ship or a boat. And "workways with the wind and the waves" denotes turning a ship so that it maintains its balance and does not capsize during a storm.

Gospel principles are for me and you what a helm is to a ship. Correct principles enable us to find our way and to stand firm, steadfast, and immovable so we do not lose our balance and fall in the raging latter-day storms of darkness and confusion.

We have been blessed abundantly in this general conference to learn about eternal principles from the Lord's authorized servants. Now, our individual responsibility is to govern ourselves according to the truths of which they have testified.[13]

Testimony

President Ezra Taft Benson taught, "For the next six months, your conference edition of the [*Liahona*] should stand next to your standard works and be referred to frequently."[14]

With all the energy of my soul, I invite all of us to learn, live, and love principles of righteousness. Only gospel truths can enable us to "cheerfully do all things that lie in our power" to press forward on the covenant path and to "see the salvation of God, and for his arm to be revealed."[15]

I know that the doctrine and principles of the gospel of Jesus Christ are the foundational sources of direction for our lives and of enduring joy in mortality and eternity. And on this glorious Easter Sunday, I joyfully witness that our living Savior is the fount from which these truths flow. I so testify in the sacred name of the Lord Jesus Christ, amen.

Notes

1. John Taylor, in *Teachings of Presidents of the Church: Joseph Smith* (2007), 284.
2. Doctrine and Covenants 42:12.
3. Doctrine and Covenants 88:78.
4. See Articles of Faith 1:1–3.
5. See Articles of Faith 1:4.
6. Doctrine and Covenants 89:3–4.
7. Dallin H. Oaks, "The Aaronic Priesthood and the Sacrament," *Ensign*, Nov. 1998, 39; *Liahona*, Jan. 1999, 45–46.
8. See Russell M. Nelson, "The Sabbath Is a Delight," *Ensign* or *Liahona*, May 2015, 129–32.

9. Russell M. Nelson, "The Sabbath Is a Delight," 130; emphasis added.

10. Russell M. Nelson, "Let God Prevail," *Ensign* or *Liahona*, Nov. 2020, 92.

11. Russell M. Nelson, "Let God Prevail," 94.

12. Doctrine and Covenants 123:16.

13. President Harold B. Lee (1899–1973) urged members to let the conference talks "be the guide to their walk and talk during the next six months." He explained, "These are the important matters the Lord sees fit to reveal to this people in this day" (in Conference Report, Apr. 1946, 68).

     President Spencer W. Kimball (1895–1985) also emphasized the importance of general conference messages. He said, "No text or volume outside the standard works of the Church should have such a prominent place on your personal library shelves—not for their rhetorical excellence or eloquence of delivery, but for the concepts which point the way to eternal life" (*In the World but Not of It*, Brigham Young University Speeches of the Year [May 14, 1968], 3).

     President Thomas S. Monson (1927–2018) reaffirmed the importance of studying conference talks. He said: "May we long remember what we have heard during this general conference. The messages which have been given will be printed in next month's *Ensign* and *Liahona* magazines. I urge you to study them and to ponder their teachings" ("Until We Meet Again," *Ensign* or *Liahona*, Nov. 2008, 106).

14. Ezra Taft Benson, "Come unto Christ, and Be Perfected in Him," *Ensign*, May 1988, 84.

15. Doctrine and Covenants 123:17.

COVID-19 AND TEMPLES

PRESIDENT RUSSELL M. NELSON

President of The Church of Jesus Christ of Latter-day Saints

My beloved brothers and sisters, we have truly had a spiritual feast. How grateful I am for the prayers, messages, and music of the entire conference. Thanks to each of you for joining with us, wherever you are.

Early last year, because of the COVID-19 pandemic and our desire to be good global citizens, we made the difficult decision to close all temples temporarily. During the ensuing months, we have felt inspired to reopen temples gradually through a very cautious approach. Temples are now being opened in four phases, adhering strictly to local government regulations and safety protocols.

For temples in phase 1, qualified couples who have previously received their own endowments can be sealed as husband and wife.

For temples in phase 2, all ordinances for the living are performed, including one's own endowment, the sealing of husband and wife, and the sealing of children to parents. We have recently amended provisions of phase 2 and allow our youth, new members, and others with a limited-use recommend to participate in proxy baptisms for their ancestors.

For temples in phase 3, those with scheduled appointments may participate not only in ordinances for the living but also in all proxy ordinances for deceased ancestors.

Phase 4 is a return to full, regular temple activity.

We are grateful for your patience and devoted service during this changing and challenging period. I pray that your desire to worship and serve in the temple burns more brightly now than ever.

You may be wondering when you will be able to return to the temple. Answer: Your temple will be open when local government regulations allow it. When the incidence of COVID-19 in your area is within safe limits, your temple will be reopened. Do all you can to bring COVID numbers down in your area so that your temple opportunities can increase.

Meanwhile, keep your temple covenants and blessings foremost in your minds and hearts. Stay true to the covenants you have made.

We are building now for the future! Forty-one temples are presently under construction or renovation. Just last year, despite the pandemic, ground was broken for 21 new temples!

We want to bring the house of the Lord even closer to our members, that they may have the sacred privilege of attending the temple as often as their circumstances allow.

As I announce our plans to construct 20 more temples, I ponder and praise pioneers—past and present—whose consecrated lives have helped to make this history today. A new temple will be built in each of the following locations: Oslo, Norway; Brussels, Belgium; Vienna, Austria; Kumasi, Ghana; Beira, Mozambique; Cape Town, South Africa; Singapore, Republic of Singapore; Belo Horizonte, Brazil; Cali, Colombia; Querétaro, Mexico; Torreón, Mexico; Helena, Montana; Casper, Wyoming; Grand Junction, Colorado; Farmington, New Mexico; Burley, Idaho; Eugene, Oregon; Elko, Nevada; Yorba Linda, California; and Smithfield, Utah.

Temples are a vital part of the Restoration of the gospel of Jesus Christ in its fulness. Ordinances of the temple fill our lives with power and strength available in no other way. We thank God for those blessings.

As we close this conference, we again express our love for you. We pray that God will shower His blessings and watchcare upon each of you. Together we are engaged in His sacred service. With courage, let us all press on in the glorious work of the Lord! For this I pray in the sacred name of Jesus Christ, amen.